MARK WISKUP

How
GREAT COMMUNICATORS
Get the Most Out of
THEIR EMPLOYEES
and THEIR CAREERS

Don't Be *That* Boss

A Business Fable

WILEY

John Wiley & Sons, Inc.

Published by John Wiley & Sons, Inc., Hoboken, New Jersey.

Published simultaneously in Canada.

For general information on our other products and services or for technical support, please contact our Customer Care Department within the United States at (800) 762-2974, outside the United States at (317) 572-3993 or fax (317) 572-4002.

Wiley also publishes its books in a variety of electronic formats. Some content that appears in print may not be available in electronic books. For more information about Wiley products, visit our web site at www.wiley.com.

Library of Congress Cataloging-in-Publication Data:

Wiskup, Mark.
    Don't be that boss : how great communicators get the most out of their employees and their careers / Mark Wiskup.
        p. cm.
    ISBN 978-0-470-48585-9 (cloth)
    1. Communication in management. 2. Interpersonal communication.
3. Interpersonal relations. 4. Supervision of employees. 5. Management. I. Title.
    HD30.3.W574 2010
    658.4'5—dc22   2009017155

Printed in the United States of America

10 9 8 7 6 5 4 3 2 1

Contents

iii

Contents

Acknowledgments

It's hard being the boss. I found that out well enough when I ran my own company for more than 15 years. But I never realized the bizarre array of stresses and dilemmas that some bosses must handle until I began speaking to CEOs and management groups for Vistage International. This opportunity to work with more than 3,000 bosses in a wide variety of industries across the United States and Canada has given me a rare insight into leadership spirit, drive, and fortitude. For this, I'm honored and grateful.

Dan Ambrosio, my editor at John Wiley & Sons, Inc., provided tremendous insight and a strong guiding hand as we designed this fable and the troubles poor Chad would encounter along the way. It was a blast working with him.

My literary agent, Bob Deforio, did a wonderful job creating the perfect give-and-take environment for Dan and I to work in. I know I'm not Bob's only author, but I'm amazed at the level of detail he's able to focus on in the miraculous process of bringing my books to publication.

I want to thank Stan Levy, the Southeast Region Managing Partner for Grant Thornton, as well as Partner Matt Dumar, also of Grant Thornton, for giving me speedy and easy-to-understand advice (for a non-financial person like me) that kept the exchanges between the characters accurate.

Finally, I've learned a lot about how to have a positive impact on employees from my 20-year friendship with Mark House, Managing Director for the Florida Division of The Beck Group. Several of the nice touches that Chad admires in Mike come right from Mark's playbook.

Introduction

Chad would be better off now if he had that nighttime mouth guard with him. The piece of molded blue plastic that stops him from grinding his teeth while sleeping might knock out some of this pain. Without it, he clenched and unclenched his jaw with growing pressure. He sat at his desk behind a closed door, slowly turning the pages in his year's 360 degree review. His face burned. The vise around his head tightened as he read leadership scores and comments from the employees he managed.

Unfortunately for Chad, however, his colleagues had all displayed a damning consistency in their anonymous assessment of his performance:

- "Poor communicator"
- "Lack of clear strategic direction"
- "Leaves us in the dark"
- "Not enough give-and-take, if any"
- "Inconsistent in approach"

Then he turned to the real heart-stopper. His boss agreed in very similar vocabulary that his team was not performing up to goal and that he was responsible.

- "At times, Chad's team lacks direction."
- "Chad struggles with low morale."
- "Higher than normal turnover needs to be addressed."

Overall, it wasn't a career-ending review; but it wasn't going to help him, either. He was safe from the grim reaper, but he definitely was not moving forward at the company—at least not based on this document. There would be little or no performance bonus at the end of the year after this report went into the file. And it would knock Chad's promotion train off the tracks for a good 12 to 24 months, if not longer.

Chad couldn't stop gnashing his upper and lower molars because something about this just didn't make sense. He knew that he was bright. Graduating at the top of his MBA class, his 3.9 in undergrad finance and, before that, a 1540 on the SAT in high school told him so. Most of all, he had been lauded for years before he became a division manager for his outstanding business acumen. He was in early, stayed late, and was always prepared. He knew he didn't have a love fest going on with his employees, but he was never accused of being unfair.

Chad is right about all those things. He is not disrespectful of his employees or purposefully manipulative. However, he rarely connects with them. And, up to this moment, that has never concerned him. He is smart, after all, and can easily display powerful business intellect, which should create all the connections he needs. He is *that* boss.

"Wow, Chad . . . I'd say you looked like crap, but that would be, you know, unfair to crap," joked his colleague Mike who had just walked into the washroom. Chad laughed, drying the cold water he splashed on his face in hopes of snapping the migraine's grip. The water didn't spruce up his reflection in the washbasin mirror. He admitted Mike was right. Chad looked pretty beat up.

After a quick glance around, he decides to take Mike into his confidence. "Just got my 360 and it was brutal. I'm reeling here. They all say I'm a lousy communicator," says Chad. "I know I'm not the 'feel-good' rock star you are, but I don't think I'm all that bad. What do you think?"

Mike and Chad are both division managers at the same privately held company. They'd started as rookies years ago at the same time and had received their promotions to "boss" status within 10 days of each other. They had different backgrounds, strengths, and approaches to their jobs. They had immediately liked each other and had become very good friends over the years. They work on the same floor in the office tower, so it's not unusual for them to run into each other several times a day.

"I think 360s are a great help when you look at the whole process," says Mike, pressing the soap dispenser and scrubbing his hands under the water. "They're not perfect, but they're useful. The downside is that some of your employees probably love this time of year because they can sit at their desks and calmly give it to you in the 360. They don't have to back it up, and there's no accountability or retribution. A few are going to be nasty just for sport. Forget about the especially mean comments. I get them, too."

Mike turns away from the washbasin and faces Chad directly. "But, look, bud, you shouldn't stop there. We've talked a lot about your team. You tell me most of them are pretty damn good. That means when they got the 360 document for you from the HR department in their Outlook mailbox, they probably sat at their computers and really concentrated on this process.

Most of them take it seriously and want to help you and the organization improve. If more than one of them is pointing to the same warts on your management hands, you've got to listen to their voices. It means you've got work to do. So do it. You're capable. This isn't the first time you've had to blast through a wall."

Chad felt immediately better, but he couldn't figure out why. Mike didn't use this opportunity to patronize him by telling him not to worry about it. He also didn't smack Chad when he was down by agreeing that Chad's communication skills did indeed suck. Instead, Mike's direct and quick washroom assessment gave Chad a boost of energy and a bit of brightness. *Mike was right*, thought Chad. *I am capable. I can improve at this*.

Mike's employees know how Chad feels. Mike found the right words quickly to help Chad succeed; and it wasn't an accident. Mike took his friend's issue seriously and worked diligently, even in a chance conversation, to express the correct words that will help Chad. This is an example of the powerful communication skills and ongoing mental discipline that make Mike a stronger boss than Chad. Mike's communication skills combined with his communication work ethic give him a tremendous advantage over other bosses, like Chad, who struggle with lackluster results.

Mike didn't waste time gloating during this brief exchange. He easily could have, because his own 360 report—which Chad was too self-engrossed to inquire about—was a much different story. Mike received strong marks in all the communication and leadership sections that plagued Chad. Mike's report was not perfect by any means; his employees and bosses both gave him lower marks and several negative comments on his time-management skills. But these were minor points in an overall outstanding 360 degree review.

Mike's team was on goal for the year in very tough times. He was receiving the credit for the division's success from those up and down the food chain. He needed to tidy up his work routine, but he already had a plan to get the coaching he needed, starting next week.

Later that night, at home with his wife, Mike chuckled at the irony in the whole washroom back-and-forth that Chad would never recognize. Chad easily dropped not so subtle allusions to his classy academic credentials regularly in conversations and meetings. This always contrasted sharply to Mike's more pedestrian higher education campus, scores, and grades. Even a rockin' B-school doesn't have all the answers, Mike told his wife.

Mike did not resent Chad's mildly patronizing academic boasting; instead he saw the value in having a bright light resource like Chad as a friend. Mike knew how sharp Chad was and didn't hesitate to ask him to weigh in on perplexing business issues he was struggling with. Chad may brag a little, but he is loyal and always happy to help Mike and others across division lines. Mike and Chad are both strong employees for the company.

Despite his lack of a top-notch business education, Mike actually has much greater potential than Chad. The 360 reviews backed up what the bosses already knew about them: that Mike's team consistently outperformed Chad's team and most of the others in the company as well. While Mike wasn't nearly as buttoned down as Chad was when it came down to the numbers and raw financial insight, he worked diligently at building valuable connections with every one of his employees—even in minor conversations.

The execs realize that Mike's whole attitude was different. They could see he prepared more for his meetings with his employees, burning more mental calories during those conversations. He always evaluated his communication performance and asked others to weigh in to help improve his already powerful skill set. He had the same approach to management meetings. None of the execs or division managers spaced out, shuffled through papers, or checked their BlackBerrys when he spoke in the boardroom. Mike owned the room when he talked.

Mike, just slightly above average in business intellect, has become a great boss by understanding that successful communication with employees and everyone else is the key to superior team performance.

Chad easily admitted Mike's strengths. He teased that Mike has an extra charisma gene that some people are just lucky enough to be born with. Chad never considered that Mike is actually working at his communication, that it's not just the gift of gab.

Poor B-school genius Chad hasn't been able to figure this out. He thinks if he just comes in a little earlier, reworks those spreadsheets, and uses stronger language in an e-mail, he can prove to his employees that he is right. Then they should do what he says, the way he says it should be done.

The next 12 chapters will chronicle, hour by hour, a mirrored day in the business life of both Mike and Chad. We'll watch them experience similar everyday communication scenarios: group meetings in a conference room, one-on-one sessions in an office, chance conversations in the coffee room, telephone calls, and even e-mail correspondence. Some of these will be high impact and obviously stressful conversations; some of them will appear to be simple, but then become complicated.

Though no two real division managers would ever have exactly parallel days, hour by hour, this story asks us to make a leap and accept that they do. In this block of simultaneous episodes during this typical business routine, we'll witness the lackluster results Chad sees by concentrating solely on imparting accurate information and reasonable directives to his employees. Mike—who, on the other hand, consciously chooses to prepare for and work to build strong connections in every interaction—will enjoy significantly more success throughout the day.

Chad's lousy 360 ruined his weekend. Monday morning, he vows he will change. He doesn't know what steps to follow to reach the business metamorphosis; but he's determined to find out.

7:00 AM

Connections Made and Missed Out of the Gate

7:05 Forgetful Mike Lucks Out

Mike weaves his way through the morning throng at the convenience store. He is headed, as usual, back to the coffee island where he will prepare his first fix of the day. Ngoc is holding court at the register—laughing, teasing with several regulars as well as newcomers. She trades newspapers, cigarettes, gum, donuts, and juice for money and debit cards with the deftness of a Monte Carlo croupier.

Without missing a beat, she also delivers a corrective shout to her employee, who is building a point of purchase display directly behind her. The tiny woman with a Beatles haircut reminds the young man that every 12-pack has to face the customer in the same way in order to meet the distributor's display diagram.

"Extra large coffee for the extra large big shot . . . that will be $2.12 for you, Mr. Big Shot," Ngoc deadpans to Mike.

"There are two reasons I come in here, Ngoc. One is the fresh coffee; the other is the dose of humility you dole out. My wife says you are the only one who can keep me in line," Mike says.

"Your wife is a paradox. She says brilliant things like that, but she still had the bad judgment to tie herself to you. Is she smart or crazy . . . huh?"

"Maybe it was just a momentary lack of judgment," Mike says as he starts to pat, pat, pat his pockets, looking for his wallet, which he isn't finding.

"Yeah, that explains it," says Ngoc, who speaks grammatically perfect English but with a heavy accent. She loves to display her hard-won command of English idioms and slang. "What's wrong, Big Shot? So many things on your important plate today you can't remember a simple thing like a wallet?"

"Geez, I'm a moron. Sorry for the trouble." Mike heads back to the coffee island to dump out his cup, mildly irritated with himself. He wants the jolt of caffeine that first cup would provide. This is exactly the type of spacey behavior his bosses and his employees had pointed out in his 360 on Friday.

"Not so fast, Big Man. Today you'll drink your coffee as a treat from me. Not a gift from the corporation, either. I'm personally going to take what little money I have out of my wallet and pay for Mr. Big Shot's coffee," Ngoc dramatically removes two ones, a dime, and two pennies from her clasp.

"Because this morning I'm the Big Shot . . . my daughter got into Cal Tech yesterday." Everyone in line cheers as Ngoc awarded Mike his coffee.

"What about Princeton? Doesn't she have an application there, too?" Mike asks, happy he could get that first sip in.

"Oh, she got the rejection from Princeton yesterday, too, but that's okay. She will go to school with others like her, who can manage only a 4.5 GPA and a 1580 on the SAT," she says with a wink.

"Princeton is more for a smarty pants like you," she jokes. "We're just humble products of the public schools in my house."

Ngoc knows better than this, though. Over the past year or so, Mike has come in just about every morning. They have developed a nice friendship, and found that despite differing cultural backgrounds, they were similar in many ways. Through simple and direct questions over morning coffee purchases, Mike has learned Ngoc ran not just one but two of these stores for the publicly traded corporation. After the morning rush, she will hustle another store to bark instructions at her competent assistant managers. Her stores are the highest grossing and most profitable ones in the district.

Mike also asked about her family. That's why he knew her daughter was an academic star who earned prestigious high school honors. Ngoc gave him weekly updates on the college application process. And Ngoc knows plenty about Mike, too. He is happy to share stories about himself as well. If the store is quiet, he'll tell her about his projects and minor losses and successes at work. He never has to go into much detail; she is a quick study. She can commiserate with him, even though she isn't familiar with his business or his customers.

Despite her constant teasing, Ngoc realizes Mike isn't just a frat boy made good. She appreciates that he worked his way through state school and takes his career and his supervision of his division very seriously. They compare notes frequently about employee issues.

"If she gets into Stanford today, can I get another free cup of coffee tomorrow?" Mike asks on the way out.

"No way, Dude," Ngoc says. "One time deal, today only. Tomorrow: no money, no coffee for the Big Shot. But she won't hear from Stanford for another week, anyway."

"Okay, tell her congrats from me." Mike hustles out, gets into his car, and shuffles his iTouch to AC/DC's "It's a Long Way to the Top (If You Wanna Rock 'n' Roll)."

Then, just like he did back in high school, he turns up the volume too loud to be considerate of others in the parking lot. He is happy for Ngoc and can't help acting out some. A little AC/DC in the morning never hurt anyone, he rationalizes as he headed for the office.

But he is still irritated about the wallet.

7:06 Dry Cleaners Disappointment for Chad

"Yes, sir, I'll get the items on this ticket right away," the lady behind the counter at the dry cleaners tells Chad. He in turn manages a polite grunt of recognition as he keeps his head down, thumbing his BlackBerry. He is dismayed by one e-mail from the West Coast that popped up. His impulse is to fire off something immediately, but, remembering Friday's critical 360, he decides to let it sit until he got to the office. Making just a sliver of eye contact, Chad hands the lady behind the counter at the dry cleaners his debit card, signs the slip, and walks out with his shirts. He jumps into his car, turns up the audio on his MP3 download of the best-selling *Freakonomics,* and congratulates himself for never letting a moment of the day go by without being productive.

The "lady behind the counter at the dry cleaners" is named Joan, but Chad doesn't know that, even though he's been a customer for years. Their discussions only cover the day's temperature or impending precipitation. She wears a large plastic nametag on her polo shirt with the store logo. He's never noticed it.

In reality, Joan is scared to death of Chad. "Intimidated" is probably a more accurate term, but it sure feels a lot like fear to Joan. With his meticulously measured conversation, hurried manner, and smart, trim fashion sense, Chad always makes Joan feel inadequate. He is obviously well educated and very successful. Chad is never rude or unkind, just uninterested.

Joan knows she is just the "lady behind the counter at the dry cleaners" to Chad, and that she shouldn't take it personally. She loves getting to know her customers and takes seriously the faith they placed in her to take care of some of their dearest possessions. She learned quickly that Chad values speed above all else, so she always bolts through his counter transactions in an effort to please him.

Usually, this attention to customer needs pays off nicely for Joan and her husband. They own this store as well as a second one in a nearby suburb. They are profitable and have nine employees. Last year, the biggest guys in town offered to buy them out at a nice price. But Joan and Bob felt they were not done with what they were building, so they politely refused.

Chad would be shocked to know that this "lady at the dry cleaners" and her husband earned more money last year than he did. They have a nice bit of net worth, as well. Even with a depressed real estate market, they are still sitting on a ton of equity in their two well-run, prime location stores.

Chad's BlackBerry vibrates in his shirt pocket. He sees it is his wife, so he turns down *Freakonomics*, jams the Bluetooth Jawbone in his ear, and clicks the on button.

"Hi honey. What's up?"

"Hey, have you been to the dry cleaners yet? I wanted to make sure you picked up a suit I brought in the other day. The lady says it would be ready by yesterday. I want to wear it to the partner lunch tomorrow."

"No, she just gave me my shirts. Did you put it in under your name, or mine?"

"Oh, I just gave her our last name."

"Well, then she should have gotten it for me. I swear to God, service people really take no pride in their work these days. Jesus!" Chad swears when he is upset—mildly though, only when he's really angry. He never drops the F-bomb. He thinks it is overused and inelegant.

"Well, honey, I really should have given you the ticket, or at least told you to ask her for the suit. Don't get so frustrated. And don't be so hard on her. They do a good job for us."

"Whatever," Chad fumes. "I'm sick and tired of people doing just enough and, God forbid, not one bit more than they need to, just to get along. Would it have killed her to look harder for other items with our name?"

Joan at the dry cleaners would have agreed with Chad. She would also be mortified to know she had not done her best for a customer. Normally, she would have taken a minute to check the computer more carefully for other items with Chad's name. But he rattles her so much every time he comes in that she rushed through the transaction and missed the suit for his wife. She appreciates the business Chad and his wife bring to her store, and she would never want to disappoint them. But today she had.

"Get over it, babe," Chad's wife says. "It's not a big deal . . . I'll get it on the way home tonight."

"Alright, love you. See you tonight."

Chad clicks off the Jawbone and turns up the audio in his car to continue his self-improvement on the way into the office.

7:25 Chad Plays "The Big Man" in the Break Room

Once he hit the office, Chad launches into his Monday morning ritual. For about a year now he's taken up the deliberate practice of spending about 15 minutes first thing every Monday morning in the break room. He sits facing the door, sipping a fresh cup of chamomile tea with a dollop of honey, while perusing the front page of the *Wall Street Journal*.

The *WSJ* is merely an affectation. Chad would rather read it in his office. No, he is really there to greet employees and show that he enjoys touching base with them—whether or not they work for him. He believes that his being "out there" and making small talk display good leadership skills.

"Hi Lindsay, how was your weekend?" he asks the corporate receptionist who opens the refrigerator, looking for half-and-half.

"Oh, you know, busy as usual," Lindsay replies. "How was your weekend?"

"Great . . . great. Can't believe it's Monday already, though," says Chad.

"Yeah, me too. It seems like we just walked out of here on Friday afternoon. Well, have a good day." She pours the half-and-half in her coffee and turns to walk out.

"Yes, you too, Lindsay."

Chad repeats this exercise 10 times in the next 15 minutes. Turns out, everyone's weekend was "great" or "restful" or "busy." It is no different from the same shallow call and response of every other Monday.

Chad still has that disconcerting e-mail from the West Coast to contend with, but he proudly maintains vigil. He feels good about it. He demonstrates to all employees he is concerned and available.

Lindsay and the others don't think about the interaction that way, though—because they don't really think about it at all. It is too brief and meaningless to have any impact. If pressed, they might realize that Chad mans this post every Monday morning; but they never do. There is no reason to find it significant.

Undaunted, Chad calculates constantly. He likes to keep track in his head how many colleagues he greets in his Monday morning routine. There's solace in numbers and head count. The more people he greets in the break room—instead of reading the *WSJ* prop—the more credit, and perhaps productivity, he'll get during the week.

7:50 Tarantino Debate Outside Louis's Office

With his coffee room "meet and greet" assignment completed, Chad heads to his office. He approaches Mike, who is in the hallway leaving his sales manager's office. Mike is still talking to Louis, who is hidden from Chad's view. "Well, you make a good case for it, but *Jackie Brown's* not going to go in my Netflix queue. For the last 10 years I've been hearing would-be hipsters like you say it's all stylistic and cool, but I find Tarantino's violence just too gratuitous. See you in the conference room in a few."

"Your loss," Chad hears Mike's sales manager try to get in the last word, "Samuel L is definitely on the top of his game every time he and Quentin team up."

Mike shoots back, "Yeah, well, I'll still feel I've lived a full life if on my death bed *Reservoir Dogs* is the only Tarantino film I've seen."

"Well, it's still my mission to broaden your limited horizons," Louis replies, as he brings an end to the banter.

Chad and Mike walk down the hall side by side. Chad asks, "Since when did you and Louis become Netflix buddies?"

"Well, we're not. He doesn't need Netflix like I do. In the last 10 years Louis has amassed this huge DVD collection. He spends every spare dime and free minute watching movies. He was a film major at NYU."

"Wow, how did he get here then . . . I thought he had an MBA in marketing?" Chad asks.

"Yeah, you're right, he does. His folks offered him a bribe when he was getting out of undergrad. He could do the starving artist thing on his own, or they would pop for business school. He says he sold out and went for the money. He protests that they forced him into being a money-grubbing Capitalist—he wasn't born into it the way I was. It's a good thing for us, huh?"

"Yeah, good thing for us," Chad murmurs. Louis is a strong employee for Mike, with lots of potential. But Chad is really wondering how the hell Mike knows so much detail about Louis's past. That stuff went back more than 10 years or so.

"Yeah, I'm just a mainstream movie guy, but my wife likes the art house stuff every now and then. When I have questions about something a little offbeat, I chat with Louis. The guy's a Roger Ebert of movie knowledge. He knows all the background: who ripped off the script ideas, how much the movie grossed, who was sleeping with whom on set. He really studies this stuff. It's a riot."

Mike does not do the Monday morning walk-around the way some bosses do. And he doesn't wait in the break room to greet employees, the way Chad does, though he would readily admit it was a nice touch, if done right. Instead, Mike has a deliberate routine on Monday morning. Coffee in hand, he makes a point to visit with one of his employees for a good 10 minutes; in their cubicles, at the copy machine, or as they are setting up for a meeting in the small conference room, he has a brief but meaningful chat about their weekend. His consistent but noninvasive questions make sure he gets details about the weekend instead of just a single adjective. Mike figures, if he can probe a little to find out what people admit they like doing, they'll know that he values them as colleagues.

Mike consciously stresses the word "value" in all of his motives at work. He wants his employees to know he appreciates their strengths and diversity of interests. If they succeed, they are providing strong value to the organization. If they fail, they aren't living up to the value he knows they're capable of. It makes all workplace conversations easier when you are constantly seeking and measuring value.

Mike abhors the word *care* when it comes to professional relationships. He thinks it's creepy sounding. Worse, if he said it to an employee, it would be a lie. He "cares" about his wife; he "cares" about his nieces; he "cares" about his Nirvana vinyl collection. But he doesn't "care" about his employees; he "values" them. It is a huge distinction for Mike. Ironically, he rarely uses the actual word *value* out loud. He knows it's more important to demonstrate the meaning of the word *value* with his hard-won connections than to talk about it all the time.

During these Monday get-togethers, he shares something about himself, as well. He wants his employees to value their connection to him. Today, in Louis's doorway, Mike had been discussing the film noir kick his wife had been on for the last few months. That led Louis to push *Jackie Brown* on Mike, and not for the first time. It was like this every Monday, just with a different employee each time. He had created a brief but effective non-work-related connection session with someone in the office.

Mike did not run into Lindsay, the corporate receptionist, this Monday morning as Chad had in the break room. Chances are he would have guessed how hectic her weekend was, though. He already knows Lindsay and her husband have to deal with a big decision regarding their 11-year-old son. The kid is an all-star striker in soccer and an overpowering pitcher in his baseball league. The soccer coach wants him to play on a statewide traveling club team. The baseball coach is pushing for a spring AAU league, which means playing around the state as well. Lindsay and her husband think doing both would tear the kid and the family apart every weekend. But all of this would be news to Chad.

Though Mike's casual Monday conversations look off the cuff, they are indeed highly calculated. They never last more than 10 minutes. He has a little mental timer in his head that starts to ring at about the eight-minute mark, telling him to wrap it up. He also never allows the conversations to stray into his employees' personal relationship issues—positive or negative. That's not his interest, and it will not help him accomplish his objective. While he may know and even inquire about a sick mother-in-law, that's not what these discussions are for. The word in the office is that Mike is a great guy, but he won't tolerate drama in any form. He focuses on activities and interests that will allow him to connect with employees in an upbeat fashion. It's a leadership exercise that takes time and patience; he's determined to make it pay off.

Mike believes that the more he connects with his employees and shows he is interested in them in an authentic yet professional way, the better performance he'll get from them. On top of that, he likes the back-and-forth that he has with them and has learned a lot along the way. The whole Louis "film professor" thing is a good example of the type of delightful discoveries these sessions have yielded. Mike has never discussed this tactic with Chad or anyone else in the company; he doesn't even consider it a deliberate tactic. It's just part of his routine to get the most from his employees.

The weekend reports from the western regions are waiting for Chad and Mike after their computers fire up at their individual offices. Chad has known about—and has been fretting over—this e-mail since the dry cleaners. While Mike knew he had received an e-mail from the server on the West Coast—as he always does on Monday morning—he, unlike Chad, hadn't opened it up on his BlackBerry to see if it was positive or negative. He knew that it would be "whatever it was." He just checked his BlackBerry to see if there were any meltdowns. His intuition was right. The West Coast e-mail was disappointing, but it was hardly a business tragedy.

Both Mike and Chad have to deal with the same issue. The reports from the West Coast are incomplete and will therefore not be helpful to what they have to accomplish today as they stand. They are going to need more information from the West Coast teams, and they're going to need it by noon. That's going to be a challenge.

Chad and Mike both have an important meeting with a critical vendor after lunch, the purpose of which is to get better pricing from the vendor in the months ahead. Without the promised sales projections from the West Coast for the next two quarters, a difficult goal will become almost impossible to accomplish. On top of that, it will be embarrassing. Why would the vendor give these guys a discount when they can't even figure out how much they're going to be buying?

7:55 Chad Strikes Back at West Coast Phil

This isn't the first time the Phil in the West Coast office had let Chad down. Phil is a good guy and a real hustler, but he's sloppy. Follow-through is not one of his strong points. Chad quickly composes a professional but terse e-mail.

Re: NEED PROJECTIONS YOU PROMISED!!!
Phil:

I can't tolerate less than complete work from you and your team. You have to be accountable to honor your commitments to us.

Just to remind you, you said you'd include your purchasing projections in your weekly report. You didn't, which has us in a real jam.

Please get those numbers to me by 9 AM your time.

I look forward to your immediate response to this critical issue.

Chad

Division Manager

Chad reads the e-mail over twice before sending it. He's still smarting from Friday's 360 and is being cautious. But, as he sees it, he is totally in the right—and Phil is totally in the wrong. No reason to tiptoe around this. He's the boss; and, in this e-mail, he's doing his job—and quite well, at that! No wasted words, just a strong directive.

7:57 Mike Picks Up the Phone

Mike received a similar type of e-mail from his West Coast manager—a woman named Jeanie. Mike had exactly the same reaction as Chad: He was angry. He composes an e-mail, similar in tone to the one Chad had just sent to Phil. Not quite so strident, and a few paragraphs longer, but with the same message. Before he hits the "send" key, he stops and deletes it.

He picks up the phone, thinks for a solid minute, and then leaves this voice message on her cell:

Hi Jeanie . . . this is Mike. Listen, I'm hoping to catch you as soon as you check your BlackBerry this morning because I need your attention right away, before you even get into the office.

I've got that vendor meeting at 1 PM this afternoon. Without your projections I'll look like an asshole, wasting his time asking for a pricing discount and favorable delivery options when I don't even know what we'll be ordering from him. I'll blow an opportunity to pick up some easy margin dollars if I'm not able to show him we're the real deal from the start to get the talks going. I can't do that without your projections spreadsheet.

Can you send it to me now? By now, I mean while you're still at home, even if you're about to get the kids off to school. I'll be in a jam without it and we'll lose money for sure, that we don't have to lose.

Let me know if you can do this.

Mike went through about five run-throughs of this voice mail in his head before he ever dialed Jeanie's number, editing and improving each version. The words he finally delivered to her voicemail were well-thought-out and designed to result in a specific action from Jeanie: She must send him the important documents right now. He also showed he understood the obstacles she would face, and that they didn't matter.

The self-description of "asshole" was not a term he spoke out of frustration. He used it to emphasize the predicament in which she had left him. It was just what Mike wanted Jeanie to hear because, without the information from her, the vendor wouldn't just think that Mike was unintelligent. It was worse than that. The vendor would assume that Mike wasn't considerate of other people's valuable time—hardly the opinion you want other people to hold when you're trying to get a concession from them. Yes, Mike thought "asshole" was the perfect word, and he wanted Jeanie to hear the concern in his voice along with the word.

This is the way Mike operates every day. He works and massages each communication that could affect his employee's behavior and performance. He'll use coarse (but not gross) language to get his point across if it's the best way to connect with his message.

Next, he turns to his computer and sends this e-mail:

Re: JUST LEFT YOU AN IMPORTANT VM YOU NEED TO CHECK RIGHT NOW.

Please to listen to the voice mail right now. I need your help on one item before you get to the office.

Thanks,

Mike

With that, both Chad and Mike head to their respective sales meetings. Both think to themselves that the day isn't off to a bad start at all. Could be better, but they had already taken care of business, caught a problem early, taken action, and were headed for a pretty good day.

Only one of them would be right.

7:00 AM

Don't Be That Boss Lessons

7:05 Forgetful Mike Lucks Out

✓ Seek to build connections all day long without evaluating whether or not it will pay off for you professionally.

7:06 Dry Cleaners Disappointment for Chad

✓ Missed connections add up to productivity losses and frustration.

(continued)

(*continued*)

7:25 Chad Plays "The Big Man" in the Break Room

✓ Low energy and low investment communications yield little, if any, return.

7:50 Tarantino Debate Outside Louis's Office

✓ Taking the time to find out nonintrusive details about employees and colleagues demonstrates a real interest and value in the professional relationship.

7:55 Chad's Strikes Back at West Coast Phil

✓ Speed is the crafty enemy of successful communication.

7:57 Mike Picks Up the Phone

✓ Slowing the pace and delivering well-thought-out communication will result in better performance.

8:00 AM Sales Rundown:

Reality Behind the Numbers

8:01 Chad Admires His Handiwork

Chad glows every Monday morning as he sits in Conference Room A, studying the format and layout of the sales report for his division. He's proud of his creation. This homegrown report displays a brilliant snapshot of his sales team's performance. And that's not just his opinion. Other division bosses and senior management at the company have praised the way Chad cobbled together this succinct, powerful combination of spreadsheets and graphics.

This morning, he beams again at his baby. This reporting mechanism was originally a duty for his sales manager, Jody. She put together a functional set of spreadsheets after Mike made the request, well within the deadline they agreed upon. But it was a very vanilla way to track sales progress. It took Chad and his team 20 to 30 minutes of rigorous discussion in these Monday sales meetings to figure out where everything stood.

Chad isn't disappointed in Jody for creating such a pedestrian reporting mechanism. Spreadsheet manipulation is not a part of her job description, and it isn't in her core competency. Jody's strength is her insight into the sales process, and Chad depends on her judgment. Though Chad has a severe weakness in his leadership communication skills, no one complains that he's unfair. He's not one to force unrealistic expectations upon his employees.

There was no reason to chide Jody for her report. Still, he felt his division and his company deserved something more dynamic. So he decided to take the initial spreadsheet template from his sales manager and make it sing. Jody didn't mind. She, along with everyone else, realized Chad was a wiz.

He unveiled his new creation after just a few weeks of sweat during early morning hours and between appointments. Using detailed formulas, tie-ins, and some heavy duty math knowledge spread across a wide variety of cells, he created a customized, brilliant sales activity tracking tool. The result is a simple, clear, and dynamic spreadsheet and graphic report that helps anyone, even those who don't work in his division, to understand the progress of each sales team member and each prospect in the sales activity process. Chad quantified all of the ongoing sales activities, from cradle to grave, with color codes for each grouping. The report cross-references every member of Chad's sales team member with every task they are responsible for. There's a running month-to-date, year-to-date percentage, and the actual numbers total for each activity total against budget figures for the division. It's the result of a deep set of formulas and databases

Chad has created. The final pages of the report contain a series of pie charts and graphics that make the numbers jump off the pages. They look great, not cheesy, and are easy to grasp. Chad's team members keep track of all their activities, sometimes by the hour, on his report. It's easy to use.

When Chad completed this super-template earlier in the year, he had everyone buzzing. The automation and the sophisticated reports looked like something you'd get from a massive customer relationship software project that would have cost at least six figures in consultant fees and taken a year or more to implement. That's why the company never invested in this type of stuff, even though they knew the result would be very helpful.

Chad, the brainiac at software and business measurement tools, is now in the process of helping all the other departments copy his success—all during his off time. He's happy to do it. Sure, it makes him look good, but that isn't the biggest reason Chad is pleased that his sales tracking spreadsheet is being implemented. His system is brilliant because it is efficient, and Chad loves efficiency.

Flipping through the pages, he can't help patting himself on the back. He knows he shouldn't keep congratulating himself; but damn, this is some good stuff. Chad looks forward to his 8:15 sales meeting, which, of course, he is 14 minutes early for.

8:13 Mike Is Behind Schedule, Again

Chad's cool sales template hasn't been created for Mike's division yet. The big bosses don't want to abuse Chad's goodwill and desire to help others. So the implementation of his innovative program is moving slowly through the company. That means Mike is going over his very ordinary sales reports that he and Louis created. The members of his team file into Conference Room B. Everyone takes a seat, laughing and joking, as usual.

Mike should have been there in his conference room a little earlier, or at least studied the report before this. He kicks himself again, the second time this morning, for not being prepared (the wallet and the coffee was the first time). Less than 72 hours ago, during his 360, his employees and bosses gave him a clear directive to tidy up his act. Less "seat of the pants" leadership is one of the comments he remembers.

Now Mike has fallen behind already. As a result, he has a lot of unanswered questions about the data he sees. Keeping his head down, he studies quickly and is ready for the meeting. He recovers from not budgeting the time to look at the sales report earlier. This is the reason Chad likes to call Mike "Golden Boy." It isn't that he doesn't fail: He does. But he always seems to recover so quickly.

8:15 Chad Would Die if He Knew About This Bet

Chad stands up from his seat and calls the meeting to order. No one else in the conference room has taken a seat yet. They know better. Someone told Chad a few years ago that, back when Rudy Giuliani was the mayor of New York, he had his entire staff stand during every morning briefing. Chad loved the idea immediately. He made no secret of the fact he thought sales people whined too much in meetings about client's objections. He wanted more discussion of results to get the numbers where they needed to be.

So, when Chad became boss of the division, he had everyone stand up around the table, chairs pushed aside, during the weekly sales meeting. The unspoken rule was you could sit down before the sales meeting, like Chad had done reading the report, but you had to stand up once Chad did. However, in practice, no one on the sales team wanted to take a chance on crossing Chad. So, even if they got in the room a minute or two early, they just stood and made some quiet small talk. There wasn't much good karma in the room, but it was very official looking.

Chad opens with some upbeat comments about the first four color-coded parts of the report. All the steps leading up to the initial prospect calls are right on track for this quarter, and the prospective qualification quadrant showed great activity last week, which means that the team is ahead of projections. They did their homework and now have plenty of leads to pursue. Chad goes over this quickly and then looks up from his sheets and pauses.

He's still smarting from last Friday's 360. He'll show them he knows how to be a good leader and that he cares about their success.

"Great job, guys, on the sales prep activity. This is very helpful. Thank you for your hard work," Chad smiles. He meant it.

Maryellen jabs Paul, who is standing next to her. She turns her head slightly and whispers, "No whipped cream on the Mocha Frappuccino this morning, but you can still make sure it's a Grande."

"Whatever," Paul returns under his breath. "Stop hustling me with Chad's meetings. I'm tired of losing. It's not fair. You've got some type of psycho Chad radar."

Maryellen turns slightly to Paul and winks—not coquettish, but cocky and arrogant. It is an "I own you" wink.

Everyone in the division knows Chad is furious about his 360 on Friday. He's never circumspect about his performance reviews. A competitive guy doesn't hide it when things are going well or poorly for him—he reasons. Therefore, Maryellen and the others could predict Chad would use the words "thank you for your hard work" in the sales meeting at some point in time. It's his feel-good catch phrase for when he feels the need to demonstrate that he is a caring boss. He'd never back it up with specifics of the toughness of the challenge someone had overcome. He just smiles broadly and says the generic "thanks for your hard work" when he sees a number that pleases him.

They all had heard it over and over again, so many times that it had become meaningless, and even funny, to them. When he was out of earshot, they would mimic Chad.

"Thank you for your hard work on those copies, Bill; they are really collated well."

"No, no, no . . . *thank you,* Stuart, for your hard work in washing your hands before you came out of the restroom. I'm glad you know hygiene is important." Everyone nearby would laugh.

This morning, as they were getting set in their cubicles, the playful Maryellen boldly predicted to Paul that Chad would say "thank you for your hard work" within 120 seconds of the start of the meeting. Paul agreed that Chad would default to the meaningless phrase soon enough, but he couldn't imagine he'd cough it up that quickly. It was just too transparent, even for Chad, who could never be accused of subtlety when it came to boss-employee communication.

Maryellen and Paul shook hands, sealing the bet. To the victor, a Grande drink from Starbucks of the winner's choosing. A few minutes later in the conference room Paul held up his watch ever so slightly, allowing Maryellen to see it. He clicked on the stopwatch function as soon as Chad stood up, signaling the start of the meeting. At 94 seconds, Chad belted out his encouragement cliché; and Paul knew he would be buying this morning. Maryellen cheered her insight into Chad's management style. Neither of them focused on the sales process of their division.

8:18 Wins and Losses for Mike's Team

Louis calls the sales meeting to order. Mike doesn't run his sales meeting; Louis, his sales manager, does. Louis sits at the head of the table every week. Mike positions himself at the side of the table, usually toward the end away from Louis, in a different position every week. Louis doesn't have sales prep information that Chad's team has access to, so there is no discussion of it. They usually go over all leads information once a quarter, whereas Chad's team covers it every week. Mike knows what Chad is doing, and he envies the information about leads. Once they had the benefit of Chad's template, they would look at it weekly and adjust.

This isn't Louis's fault. In the past year since Mike became the boss, he never emphasized the possible prospect or lead "universe" part of the sales process for his division. He felt what they had in place worked well enough for now and could be tweaked later. Instead, he coached Louis to focus on bringing home current prospects and proposals. Mike told the team they'd attack stronger prospecting measurement tools in the months ahead. Now, the entire focus was on turning proposals into contracts.

This concentration worked. Mike's division had strong sales, even minor growth, despite the economy. And he admitted he would have even better performance with a stronger early stage sales preparation process. Organization is one area Mike needs to work on. He lets too many important tasks, seemingly minor ones, slip between the cracks.

"Okay, wins and losses this week," Louis belts out, nodding toward Dave. "Go ahead, Dave."

"Well, as for wins, we had a great meeting at Freed-Johnson. It was very positive all the way around. They seem to really like us and what we can do for them. We were there for an hour and a half. It was a great meeting," Dave smiles. "As for negatives, we did not get short-listed on TransBell. No shock there, but I was hoping they would give us a shot."

"Okay, Gina, you're up."

"Win: We closed on Duo Canal. Didn't get quite the price we wanted, but a win nonetheless. We were at an impasse for about 15 uncomfortable minutes and then I suggested we meet in the middle. They agreed and it's done," says Gina as everyone gives an exaggerated golf clap—part of the culture Louis brought to the sales meetings. Louis knows it's important to recognize success, but he finds rah-rah cheering or bell ringing patronizing for bright professionals. The semi-facetious golf clap does the trick. It's fun and lighthearted. Everyone looks forward to giving as well as receiving the sales golf clap.

"As for a loss, we've got a one-quarter delay on Perkins. They want to make sure they get paid from a major client that's piled up a large balance before they go ahead with us . . . disappointing . . . . I thought we'd have it as a bigger win than Duo Canal. We're stuck 'doing the time warp again.' There's nothing we can do."

Gina's report pleases Mike and Louis. She has a win that is real and a disappointing delay that she acknowledges. Both are important to the performance of the team. Recognizing that

Perkins is dead in the water for now means Gina will waste no effort chasing this prospect for a month or so. This realization will help her to focus on closable prospects.

Also, Gina made a good call with Duo Canal. Louis allowed Gina and everyone on the team the leeway to make pricing decisions in the field: on-line, real time, whatever the buzzword was, with the clients. They would still make a reasonable margin on this deal, despite the fact she lowered the price.

One by one, all six members of the sales team give a 60-second "wins and losses" report. This sets the tone for the following full-fledged rundown of all the closes, proposals, and meetings, as well as the upcoming activity for this week. To a visitor, this weekly routine looks casual and easy flowing; but it's actually tightly planned. Mike pushed for all his meetings to start with headlines and then proceed to the details. After they deliver the headlines, each salesperson has four to five minutes apiece to go over their activities in greater depth. Mike taught Louis the protocol, and Louis adopted the format, then he added his own touches, like the golf clap.

8:26 Chad Worries About Phil on the West Coast

Chad glances at his BlackBerry for the tenth time in the last 14 minutes. He's learned to turn the thing on silent, and he's stopped pounding on it in meetings after a strong bust in the chops from his boss last year. Lynne, his boss, told him in front of the other district managers "No e-mailing in meetings, Chad . . . . Your inattention to me and everyone else is sucking the life out of this room." The situation was embarrassing. He learned his lesson.

Certainly no harm, however, in keeping it on the conference table at one of his meetings, just within his line of sight. He doesn't even have to touch it to see the messages pop up; and there is nothing from Phil yet. Sure, it is only 5:26 AM Pacific time, but he was hoping Phil might have been up early and responded to that terse e-mail.

8:27 Jeanie Gets the Info to Mike

The tinny BlackBerry ring tone of Mozart's "Eine Kleine Nachtmusik" fills Mike's empty office for 18 seconds before voice mail clicks in. Earlier he slipped his BlackBerry in the docking cradle, next to the computer. Mike never brings his BlackBerry to meetings in the office. Instead, he carries a mole-skin notebook and a hardcover bound calendar. Unlike almost every other manager in the company, he isn't addicted to his "CrackBerry." While he loves having the powerful communications tool, he doesn't find it helpful—as so many others do—to have it at his side every second. It isn't some protest against the intrusion of technology; he just feels that checking e-mail more than four times a day is terribly inefficient. He also learned that it ruined his focus and his ability to succeed in meetings.

Here's the voice mail Mike will hear in a few minutes when he returns to his office:

Hi Mike, this is Jeanie. I'm at my computer right now, sending you the rest of our projections for next year. I'm sorry you had to call and remind me. There are many reasons I didn't get it to you, but none of them matter. I owed it to you, and now here it is. Have a good meeting with that guy, and don't let him think you're an asshole—at least about this. Please drop me a note and let me know you got the e-mail. If I don't hear from you in an hour I'll call you again. Please accept my apology for this. See ya.

A minute or two later, the e-mail with the projections will hit the Outlook Inbox on Mike's computer. A minute after that, it appears on his Blackberry.

8:27 The Numbers Mislead Chad

As his sales team discusses what they did last week and what they have coming up, Chad carefully measures all sales activity against the numeric goals outlined in his outstanding report template. Every time the right number hits the goals on his spreadsheet he gives a proud thumbs-up. If not, he usually says something obvious like, "We're off goal. We have to hit our numbers to succeed." His sales team members nod. They agree; they just don't know what exactly Chad thinks they should be doing to get to the goal.

Today he's not happy with the number of proposals in the pipeline and upcoming initial meetings. However, he notes that formal closes are right on the money for the month, so it's easy to be encouraging. He thanks all in the room for their hard work—for the second time—and dismisses them.

But Chad's sales manager, Jody, thinks that he made a mistake in concluding the meeting so quickly. Chad called one thing right: It was a good week for closes, and for that Jody is happy. But she knows the weak pipeline is trouble. She has a good nose for the sales process and worries the division is off track more than Chad realizes. Some of those proposals, already too few in number, are probably less real than the members of the sales team owned up to. She sweats the fact that more than a few have less than a 50 percent chance of succeeding. Future actual revenue won't keep pace with what today's projected close numbers show. Jody knew some questions would help get to the real number. But she didn't interject; and Chad didn't ask her to offer an opinion.

Maybe, she thought, *Chad didn't want to rock the boat this morning.* Even if that's the case, she thinks that he made the wrong call. *With the division already behind, any sense of good karma right now is misleading, and any problems should be addressed immediately. If she ran the sales meetings, she would never let overly positive proposals or "full of crap" prospect meetings go unchallenged.* She'll talk to Chad later in the week with her concerns. He'll probably agree with her.

Unfortunately that means that she'll have to circle back with several members of the team in a few days to get the right info and remind them to commit only to what's a strong prospect. She knows it will be a waste of time as well as a couple of lost days of the week. Under stronger leadership, this waste of effort could be eliminated.

8:52 Mike Busts Dave

It isn't until the end of the meeting that Louis turns to the tabulation of the headlines and reports into a numbers format. Louis always closes by delivering a few headlines of his own. "It was a good week," Louis says. "We can always do better, and that's what I expect. So go after it this week, and remember, my door is open and my cell phone is on every minute of every day."

Then Louis turns to Mike, who frequently asks some block-and-tackle questions just to get a better feel for each prospect and customer. Other times his questions are probing in an attempt to make sure his team is delivering the information to measure real success.

This week, his calm and straightforward digging also uncovers something about Dave's activity that Louis should have caught.

"Dave, who did you meet with at Freed-Johnson?" Mike asks, following up on Dave's proclamation of a "win" as the meeting started.

"Um, it was with the purchasing manager and the head of the production department," Dave says.

"Do you think they have sign-off approval? I mean, if we get to the proposal stage, will we have to start all over again, up the food chain with the real decision makers?" Mike asks. He thinks he knows the answer, but he isn't sure.

"Well, they told us they'd probably have to get the division VP or, even better, the CFO in another meeting to even get to the proposal stage, but they were optimistic they could make that happen," Dave answers. Mike's gut was right. This isn't a "win," according to Mike's litmus test. It's just the type of consistent activity needed to get to a win.

"This was a really good start, though," Dave coughs up another overstatement, still trying to rescue the situation. He takes another breath and decides to go with a new tactic: full disclosure, knowing that Mike will get there anyway.

"But I don't know when we'll get to the CFO," Dave fesses up. "I've already called her and dropped her an e-mail. She's pretty busy, though, and it's not easy to get on her calendar."

"Okay, thanks Dave," Mike says evenly. He offers no criticism or negative response to Dave's explanation.

But that doesn't stop everyone in the room from looking down for a painful few beats because this is a lousy moment for both Dave and Louis. Dave, like everyone on the sales team, knew better than to call something that was just normal activity a "win." Mike lectured over and over again that these kinds of meetings—the type that may or may not pan out—are not "wins." "It's a pretty chord," Mike would say, "but that's not the same as a pretty song." If Dave had a meeting with the CFO at Freed-Johnson, it would have counted as a win. That's a very hard meeting to get and reason for celebration.

Most of the division managers, like Chad, take for granted that their salespeople's actions will follow the money. Why would a boss waste so much time or energy pushing people who get a bigger check when they succeed, they'd wonder. If salespeople were true professionals, the school of thought goes, it should be obvious they need closes, not just meetings.

Mike, however, doesn't agree. He sees the "they will always follow the money" argument as a misguided and lazy management style for a boss. He creates extra steps of verbal infrastructure in all of his sales meetings with his staff. The boss—Louis, in this instance—needed to question and closely monitor salespeople and keep them on the right course. For Mike, constant coaching and guidance are always more helpful to success than just incentive pay. This is one of the reasons that Mike's division met and then exceeded sales goals every one of the last four quarters.

Dave probably had a lousy week, though, and didn't have a "win" to report; so he tried to make something sound better than it was. Mike knows salespeople do this all the time. Dave would have been better off admitting he had no wins this week.

Louis is in worse shape than Dave. As sales manager, he should have caught Dave's public overselling of the Freed–Johnson meeting. Mike only pushes with these questions in front of the entire group when his internal sales radar screams that something doesn't smell right. Sometimes, his radar is off and a "win" is really a "win." That's fine with Mike because it teaches his sales people to be clearer with the reality behind the headlines.

The closes from last week are all real, which is cause for minor celebration, but Mike can see the upcoming proposal pipeline is weak. This is bad news, and everyone in the room knows it from Mike's piercing question.

8:54 Chad Is Still Sweating About the West Coast

Chad's a little nervous about Phil's lack of a response. He knows Phil gets up early, because of the time difference. He thinks of firing off another e-mail, tougher than the first, but he stops, thinking it might make him look weak. Too late, though.

8:59 Mike Gives Louis a Leadership Lesson or Two

After the meeting breaks up, Mike spends his usual five minutes of postmortem with Louis. It's a weekly, scheduled coaching session, meant to help Louis, who is a good sales boss, to become even better. Today, Louis knows he screwed up.

"Sorry I didn't catch the Dave thing before you did. I'm really excited about the Freed-Johnson prospects, and I got too caught up in it," Louis explains.

"I know. . . I am too. The reason we have such tight rules for the win/loss exercise is to make sure we keep moving forward. It's lousy discipline to pat ourselves on the back for stuff that's not significant yet," Mike says. "I'd have been more happy hearing Dave's Freed-Johnson during his five-minute report of normal activity."

"I should have caught it," Louis says.

"Yeah, you should have. I loved busting chops in sales meetings, listening to the crap and catching it early before we wondered why we weren't hitting our goals. But unfortunately for me that's your job here, not mine," Mike says. "We both look bad when I have to back you up like that. But I will, every time."

"You're right," Louis says.

"Okay, now a more subtle point I want you to work on. You were correct in complimenting them at the end of the meeting; it was a good week, and your directness worked well. But that 'we can always do better' and 'that's what I expect' stuff sounds like something you saw on an inspirational poster kiosk at the mall. You have to be more specific with what you want other than 'better.' It's too vague to show leadership."

"Well, I don't know exactly what I want, but I know I want better performance," says Louis. "Doesn't everybody?"

"Yeah, of course," Mike explains, "but if you can't put some thought and effort into 'better'—like pinpointing a specific client you've been coveting, a record number of wins in a week, or whatever—then you just sound hollow and weak. It's not that 'I expect you to do better' is bad; is just that it's average boss blah-blah-blah. You are not average, Louis. Work harder next week at developing an above average closing to the meeting."

"Okay," says Louis.

"One more thing," Mike says. "Please don't use the 'my door is always open' line ever again. Sounds too much like something Mike Brady would say to Bobby after a real father-to-son chat in the study."

Mike smiles, and Louis does, too. They split off into their separate directions, with Louis wondering if he'll ever be able to see things as clearly and word them as succinctly as Mike can. Mike knows he dropped the hammer down pretty hard on Louis; at the same time, he knows it was the right thing to do. Louis is bright and coachable. Mike is always coaching, even with his best employees. He's confident Louis will incorporate some of his tips next week.

8:00 AM

Don't Be That Boss Lessons

8:01 Chad Admires His Handiwork

✓ Do not perform work that you should be delegating or you will hamper organizational development as well as efficiency.

8:13 Mike Is Behind Schedule, Again

✓ Don't let yourself off the hook. Constantly evaluate your own performance. Admit poor leadership activities and hone in on what must be improved.

(continued)

(continued)

8:15 Chad Would Die if He Knew About This Bet

✓ Shallow praise is patronizing; nonspecific praise is worse than no praise at all.

8:18 Wins and Losses for Mike's Team

✓ Spend more time coaching star players than weak players. Strong players will take your coaching and add their own touches to create even better outcomes.

8:26 Chad Worries About Phil on the West Coast

✓ Concentrate always on the meeting you are in at the moment. Don't let addictive technology damage your productivity.

8:27 Jeanie Gets the Info to Mike

✓ Slow down to make a strong and well-thought-out case for employee directives. This leads to better performance.

8:27 The Numbers Mislead Chad

✓ Data is meaningless unless it can be accompanied by a detailed explanation as to how it adds value to the organization.

(continued)

8:52 Mike Busts Dave

✓ Give employees the freedom to fail, and follow with corrective coaching when they do. Great bosses can coach by doing nothing more than asking a strong and simple question.

8:54 Chad Is Still Sweating About the West Coast

✓ Knee-jerk e-mails sent off without spending several moments in thoughtful consideration do not result in better performance, just more worry.

8:59 Mike Gives Louis a Leadership Lesson or Two

✓ Do not let a coaching moment pass. It is the only way to help good employees become even better.

9:00 AM Financial Reports:
A Star Is Born

9:01 West Coast Frustration for Chad

No word from Phil yet, and that has Chad a little antsy. The West Coast guys were always up and checking their BlackBerrys by now, in case there was a 911 from the mothership; and Chad's earlier e-mail would definitely qualify as a 911. He thinks it should have prompted some type of response. Chad needs to know that Phil got the message and that spreadsheet with the West Coast projected orders will be on the way soon.

Chad's first inclination is to fire off another e-mail. He turns to his computer and composes a second e-mail to Phil.

Subject: WHERE ARE YOU?
Phil. My earlier e-mail made it abundantly clear I need to hear from you . . . now. Please respond.
Chad

But he doesn't send the e-mail. He doesn't even pull up Phil's e-mail address to fill in the "To:" line. He decides to think some more about this. It's a wise decision.

Chad makes a quick analysis: Either something is wrong in Phil's personal life, Phil is pouting, or even worse, messing with him.

Oh screw it. I'll just call him, Chad thinks.

Then Chad puts the phone down. He doesn't want to appear either needy or weak, so he decides to wait it out for Phil. This is a poor decision.

9:10 West Coast Jeanie Comes Through

Back in his office, Mike checks his e-mail. He's happy to see a response from Jeanie along with an attachment.

Re: Re: JUST LEFT YOU AN IMPORTANT VM YOU NEED TO CHECK RIGHT NOW.

Mike: Here's the spreadsheet with the projections. I'm sorry. I should have had it to you when I said I would. Will you please drop me a note to let me know you got it? Otherwise, I'll call you at 10 AM, your time.

Thanks,

Jeanie

Mike opens the attachment and sees precisely the projections he needs to add to his report for the vendor negotiations this afternoon. Jeanie was late, but with a strong nudge from Mike, she performed in plenty of time.

Mike is pleased for two reasons. First of all, Jeanie understood the full importance of his message and therefore acted promptly to right her wrong. And she did it with a perfect apology. Mike taught his managers to accept responsibility for lousy performance promptly and then make amends quickly and powerfully. Finally, he wanted them to move one. "Express remorse and act upon it quickly," he'd say, "but don't wallow in it."

"Now, *this* is accountability," Mike says out loud with false sincerity. Lots of managers in the company went on and on about the importance of accountability. They threw the word around so much, Mike thought it lost all meaning, if it ever really had any at all.

That's why he was pleased with Jeanie's e-mail and even smiled when he retrieved the voice mail. She flat out said the magic words that made for the best apologies:

> *I'm sorry you had to call and remind me. There are many reasons I didn't get it to you, but none of them matter. I owed it to you, and now here it is. Good luck with the vendor today. Please let me know how it goes. I'm sorry I didn't get this to you when I said I would.*

Mike had taught all of his employees his three-tiered format to owning up to a mistake:

1. Say you are sorry—but *only* if you are sorry.
2. Don't give an excuse. If you're sorry, it means you didn't do something you were supposed to do.
3. Do whatever is reasonable to make it right.

No one who was late for a morning meeting with Mike would ever dare to blame traffic, weather, or a power outage that killed the clock radio; and anyone who didn't know better would face a blistering series of questions that always resulted in the guilty party admitting they were late because they had not allocated their time properly.

Mike walks the walk. When he screws up, he goes through the three steps himself. All of his managers had seen him do it more than once during the past few years. That's why Jeanie's voice mail apology worked so well for Mike. It was direct and short, offering no excuse. She also didn't make more of it than it was—a slight screwup, not a hanging offense. She even joked about Mike's use of the word "asshole," which showed Mike she got the message, but that she wasn't intimidated by his language.

Mike is in a buoyant mood as he heads into the small conference room for the division financial update from his controller. He notices he is two minutes early for the meeting. *Good job, Mike*, he thinks to himself.

9:13 Why Mike Likes the Financial Stuff

The senior leadership at Mike and Chad's company provides each operating division with plenty of autonomy, even though many of the divisions are housed in the same building. Each division has their own infrastructure, including a president (Chad, Mike, and others), financial controller, HR department, and IT gurus, as well as separate sales teams and production units. The big bosses set this up for two reasons. The first was the desire for each division to be as nimble as some of the stand-alone companies they compete against. This full infrastructure approach gives each division the ability to make faster decisions in response to customers' needs and pressure from competition. They are quick responders because they don't have to run everything through corporate.

This plan also gives the corporate leadership the ability to measure the performance of each division against each other easily and quickly. The constant evaluations make for an exciting and dynamic culture. They like to pick apart what each division is doing right and doing wrong, and then offer those best practices to the company as a whole—just as they did with Chad's tremendous sales tracking tool.

Mike enjoys the financials update meetings with Ellen, his controller. While he has little interest in the mechanics of accounting and cash flow, he knows how critical they are to the success of his division. He's a marketing guy, not a finance guy, but he appreciates the intricacies of how the accounting world works, all the little rules and standards. And, because of the corporate structure, he doesn't have to wait to find out how he's doing from the CFO's office. Ellen can tell him.

9:14 Phil Blasts Back at Chad

A second reminder notice for Chad's meeting with his controller pops up on his screen. He snatches his trusty BlackBerry and notepad and stands up from his desk, when he sees the e-mail from Phil appear. It isn't the response Chad had anticipated.

Re: Re: NEED PROJECTIONS YOU PROMISED!!!
Chad:

Got your e-mail this morning, and I have to tell you it caught me a little by surprise. I do remember promising my purchasing projections, but I had no idea you needed them this morning. I was planning on going over them and getting the spreadsheet out to you by Wednesday. Now, for the first time, I know you need them today.

I have a breakfast meeting with a client that I can't cancel. I'll move everything else around this morning and hopefully I can have the projections off to you by 9:30 AM my time. You shouldn't count on seeing it any earlier.

Chad, I'm sorry for the mix-up on this, but I did not know the urgency of these numbers. I would never let you down on purpose, and I think my track record shows this.

I hope you will have a successful meeting with our vendor.
Phil

This is a bad e-mail in so many ways for Chad. The worst news, of course, is that he won't have the numbers in time for the meeting with the vendor. He'll either have to cancel, show up late, or go in unprepared. Every one of the options will hurt his cause.

In addition, Chad is furious that Phil failed to acknowledge accountability for his missed assignment. Phil even had the gall to toss it off as a "mix-up." What crap! Chad knows that he had specifically told Phil about the projections deadline.

But that still isn't the worst thing about the e-mail. Phil had raised the stakes considerably by CCing Lynne, including her in the e-mail trail so that she could see Chad's original e-mail as well as the response. Lynne is the corporate executive VP and Chad's boss.

Chad feels a direct punch in the gut. Phil called Chad out in front of Lynne, and he had never pulled such a shenanigan before. On top of that, he had the political sense and even the guts to copy Lynne instead of blind copying her. A scenario in which Chad wouldn't see the correspondence going to Lynne would have been sneaky, and Lynne would have busted Phil for a devious end-around. But a direct CC wasn't devious at all—it was a full-on frontal assault.

Boy, he must be really pissed off by my by earlier e-mail, Chad thought. Free-spirited Phil and the organized Chad had endured plenty of go-arounds before, but they had always settled matters peacefully. And Phil is no dummy. He deliberately chose to make this e-mail a huge corporate issue.

The e-mail trail makes Chad look like a lousy boss—one who can't succeed with even the simplest of leadership communication exercises. So much so, his employees are now choosing to escalate issues up the corporate ladder. More fuel to that burning 360 fire from Friday.

He realizes something critical as he rereads the exchange. Phil's tone was consolatory and polite, and he offered a reasonable—if not perfect—solution to the tough situation. Chad now realizes that the words in his own e-mail, dashed off with so much authority two hours earlier, were dogmatic and almost childish. Insightful Lynne won't have to think too hard to see that Phil was sending a message: "Please, look at what we have to deal with, Lynne." This whole exchange makes Phil appear as the sensible one, while Chad comes off as the petulant child.

Chad quickly e-mails John, his controller, and asks for a 15-minute delay. He needs to think about all this; otherwise he won't be able to concentrate on the scheduled financial meeting.

9:15 Mike Likes "Apples to Apples"

"Before we get going, there is something important I need to tell you," Mike says to Ellen, with a mock serious tone.

"Oh, I'm sure there is." Ellen hands Mike the financial reports, puts her copies down in front of her, and looks right at him. "Well, what is it?" She's challenging him in this weekly game, very well aware of what's coming next.

"I had some dreams," Mike says.

Ellen shakes her head in disbelief and smiles. "Well, I guess they were just clouds in your coffee."

"Yes, they were clouds in my coffee," Mike reaffirms.

"Well, I guess someone you know is 'so vain' then, aren't they?" Ellen says.

"Nicely done!" Michael is again impressed with Ellen's prowess.

"Well, I try." Ellen is happy, too, though she knows Mike didn't work very hard on this one. But she always enjoys these little lyrics tests that Michael springs on her.

"Okay, well, what do you have for me?" Michael picks up the financial reports. The pleasantries are over with; the meeting is now officially starting.

"Well, first of all, the report today will be in a slightly expanded version," Ellen says. "I've taken our year-to-date numbers and added a comparison to benchmark numbers for our industry from several databases on the Internet. It's not a perfect comparison, but I'd still call it apples to apples, but not Red Delicious apples to Red Delicious apples. The bottom line, Mike, is that when you look at the other guys, we're doing pretty well."

This is exactly what he likes about Ellen. She frequently does extra work or develops additional financial reports that give him greater insight into how the division is performing. They're never the result of direct instructions from Mike. Ellen just starting doing these add-on chores about six months ago, and Mike made her feel great about it. It's easy for her to find the time because his specific compliments provide her with the energy and the incentive.

"This is great, Ellen, and I'm so delighted you used the 'apples to apples' thing instead of saying people who are 'in our space,'" Mike says. "Please continue. I am still on the edge of my chair." Mike presses his managers to eliminate jargon as much as possible in all of their meetings. He lectures them, sometimes daily, that relying on technical jargon—whether financial, production, or marketing—is the mark of a weak or nondistinctive leader.

Mike wants his team to become extraordinary—not just average. He tells them the best leaders dump jargon whenever possible, replacing it with commonsense language. This requires more mental gymnastics, he admitted, but makes for more powerful meetings and discussions. He'll let them use a bit of jargon once, but if they repeat it again too soon, Mike brings down the hammer.

When Mike unveiled this policy after he had been promoted, a number of his managers—including Ellen—pushed back, "So, we have to dumb it down to an eighth-grade level all the time, even when everyone knows what we're talking about?"

Mike didn't back down. "No!" He almost raised his voice, "You have to act like you are considerate of others, and that you intend to work hard to prove your point. You accomplish that when you use less jargon and only do so when it's absolutely necessary. Don't try to save time by spewing terminology. The more that you use, the more insecure or uncaring you sound. I'm going to be relentless on this, so consider this a stern warning." He was, and they all learned to follow his jargon-free communication example.

"You know, it was a struggle to not discuss 'benchmarking in our space' more, but I knew the beating I'd take if I did," Ellen admits. "Speaking the way you want us to is difficult for me."

"I know it is," says Mike, "and your hard work is paying off. Not only do I understand your reports more easily, but Andy would probably say you sound a lot more confident along the way as well." Andy is the company CFO, and, although Ellen doesn't report to him, she works with him frequently.

9:28 Chad Goes into Deep Thought

Chad makes very good use of the 15 minutes of breathing room he bought by delaying the next meeting with John, his financial guy. First of all, Chad figured out how he would handle the supplier situation. He'd just go ahead and make his pitch for better pricing without the numbers from the West Coast. He'd fake it and try to win with charm instead of numbers and data . . . and logic. It wasn't the most comfortable play for him, but he determined it was better than canceling the meeting.

Second, he composed a quick e-mail to Lynne to make sure she didn't feel the need to become a part of the little fracas with Phil.

Re: Re: NEED PROJECTIONS YOU PROMISED!!!
Lynne:

Sorry about the fact this hit your desk. I'll take care of this with Phil. I'll keep you in the loop and let you know how we resolve it.

Thanks,

Chad

He deliberately chose not to follow his initial impulse to call Lynne's cell phone, interrupting her in the middle of whatever she was doing this morning, and tell her Phil was lying. Instead this e-mail is contrite, giving Lynne good, brief information. She can take the Phil–Chad confrontation off her plate for a while.

He sits at his desk and thinks about all the variables in front of him.

The day was off to a crummy start.

Following the advice Mike gave him on Friday to take other people's insight into his communication style seriously, he starts to wonder if he might actually be the one responsible for this little mess. After about 10 minutes, he puts a list together in his head of all the variables he's facing with this Phil situation.

He resolves to make this right by the end of the day—first with Phil, and then follow up with Lynne. He doesn't know how he'll do it, but he remembers Mike's encouragement. This is just another wall he'll have to burst through. *Even though, to be completely honest,* Chad says to himself, *none of this is my fault.*

9:30 Chad Makes a Good Catch

Chad feels better about the day as John gives the polite knock on the door before entering the office. The Phil issue is bad, but it is no longer a crash-and-burn situation. Financial meetings are always fun for Chad. He loves the order, the logic, and the rules of financial reports. No chance for leeway or miscommunication here. Either a number is right, or it's wrong. He welcomes the distraction.

"Hey John, how was the weekend?" Not much variance for Chad from his break-room routine.

"Oh you know, busy and too damn short." John sits down across from Chad and hands him last month's financials for the division. The report has a lot more comparison data than the one Mike and Ellen were going over. John's columns not only show performance for last month, but they have a number of other columns so Chad can see how his team did this month compared to projections for the year, industry averages, and his own running average for the last 12 months. It's all good information for any boss to have. John and Chad have a lot of beneficial discussions about the comparative data.

"I hear you on that one. Donna scheduled social stuff for us on both Friday and Saturday nights, which is a killer," Chad complains. "I was shot all day on Sunday."

Donna—whose suit was still at the dry cleaners—was a partner in a large law firm.

"Well, I guess you don't call the shots at home any more than I do these days," John offers.

"Oh, I stopped trying to call the shots a long time ago. You can't win an argument with someone who argues for a living," Chad smiles. He's proud of Donna and likes boasting about her.

"Okay, let's take a look here." Chad picks up the reports and starts his examination.

John didn't tell him his twin daughters competed in a two-day swim meet this weekend. That's what he meant when he told

Chad he was busy. But Chad didn't ask any follow-up questions, so John lets it lie. That's fine with him. Everyone knows Chad is a decent guy, but he doesn't much care to know what goes on outside the office. He'd inquire about the twins every now and then, but not with much interest. Chad could probably remember that John's girls are on some sort of swim team, if he really thought about it. He doesn't know they're talented enough to be competing in statewide meets at their young age.

"Our office supplies expenses look a little out of whack here. Do you know why they're so high?" Chad asks. He's just testing John.

"Um, no I don't. You're right, they did spike a little last month . . . in fact, they're the highest they've been this year, when you look at the year comparison. I'll have to go back and chat with Cindy over the invoices we got this month to see what happened. I didn't notice any extraordinary shipments of stuff, though, so I don't know what it is."

John isn't sweating this. It isn't a huge dollar amount. But he knows Chad will want to get to the bottom of it.

"Well, maybe we can figure it out here," Chad offers. He already has a pretty good idea why the office supplies number is so high. "Shouldn't our depreciation expenses have gone up? We took delivery on those juiced-up computers and printers the graphics department has been bugging us about, didn't we?"

He's right, as usual, thinks John. "Yeah, that's it. We probably booked it as an office expense because the whole package was less than 20,000 bucks. Good catch. I'll have Cindy move it over to fixed assets and we'll get it into the depreciation schedule."

This is typical of the way these financial meetings go. Chad has a nose for cash flow and expenses and finds stuff like this all the time. His correction will make the P&L improve this month.

They'll depreciate the expense over three years instead of taking it all this month, so they'll pick up a few bucks.

Most likely, Andy's financial team at the corporate level wouldn't have caught it, either. Chad's division is just one of several multimillion-dollar divisions that Andy has corporate financial responsibility over. This is too small of a dollar amount to hit their radar screen.

Still, Chad is happy. His financial statements will now be accurate, and that's always important.

"I'm sorry about that, Chad. Cindy knows better, and I should have seen it before you did," John says.

"No worries," Chad says, "the important thing is that we'll get it right now."

Chad is proud of himself. He caught an error and was pretty doggone nice to John in the process. All in all, the morning just got a little bit better.

John leaves the meeting thinking, once again, Chad is a pretty sharp cookie. But John didn't learn anything from the experience. Chad missed a great opportunity to explore the reason for the mistake or help John learn how to coach Cindy to make sure the divisional financial reports have the right information in the right place.

9:53 Mike Invites Ellen to Mahogany Row

Mike really likes the extra work Ellen has been putting in to make the financials more meaningful for him. It helps him to make better decisions.

"Can you make it to the corporate management meeting next week?" Mike asks. "I'd like you to present this format with the 'apple to apples' stuff to the big bosses. This is a nice piece of work and I'd like them to see it." Mike wants to reward her hard work and innovation with meaningful recognition within the company. Ellen says she would be there and thanks him.

"Oh, and one more thing, Ellen," Mike says with a straight face and another over-the-top mock serious tone, signaling the meeting is over. "What would happen next if I told you that *'you run for cover so discreet'*?" He asks, with no smile.

"Why that would be quite simple, Mike," Ellen says, admitting to herself that this reference to The FIXX is significantly more taxing than his earlier lyrical quiz about Carly Simon's "You're So Vain."

She doesn't let him know that, though. "Why, I would quickly ask *'why don't they do what you want, say what you mean?'*"

"And why," asks Mike, "Would you possibly do that?"

"Because everyone knows that *'one thing leads to another.'*" Ellen triumphs.

"Damn! Next week, I will get you," Mike jokes.

"Doubtful," says Ellen. She walks out of his office.

Yeah, doubtful, Mike thinks, filled with wonder at Ellen's financial mind and encyclopedic knowledge of '70s and '80s pop song lyrics.

9:00 AM

Don't Be That Boss Lessons

9:01 West Coast Frustration for Chad

✓ While e-mail appears to be a model for efficiency, it can also create devastating inefficiency, creating fires where none exist.

(continued)

(continued)

9:10 Jeanie Comes Through

✓ By simply taking more time to address missed deadlines and deliverables, a strong boss gets better results. He or she also gives employees the opportunity to evaluate their own poor performance and make adjustments in the future.

9:13 Why Mike Likes the Financial Stuff

✓ Understand what you are good at and what you aren't good at. Let your employees fill in the gaps and help your team to be a star.

9:14 Phil Blasts Back at Chad

✓ Overreliance on efficiency and technology in leadership communication damages your standing as a boss with your own employees—and with your bosses.

9:15 Mike Likes "Apples to Apples"

✓ Coaching your employees on their communication and other "soft skills" is just as important to being a good boss as making necessary technical corrections.

(*continued*)

9:28 Chad Goes into Deep Thought

✓ When you start to question your own role in poor team performance, you are making positive steps toward becoming a better boss.

9:30 Chad Makes a Good Catch

✓ Coach others to improve their performance, rather than just spotting and correcting their mistakes.

9:53 Mike Invites Ellen to Mahogany Row

✓ Look for ways for your employees to display their strengths to others.

10:00 AM Frustration and Satisfaction:

Strategic Plan Update

10:01 Lynn Gives Chad Some Breathing Room

As soon as John leaves the office, Chad swivels to his computer screen. He knows he's received an e-mail from Lynne. He saw it out of the corner of his eye while he was working with John, but he won the inner struggle and left his BlackBerry alone. As soon as John left, Chad whirled around to see the message from Lynne.

Re: Re: Re: SPREADSHEET

I'm glad you're on top of this. Keep me posted about what happens.

Lynne

This is *really* good news for him. Lynne is letting him know that she will stay on the sidelines, giving Chad the Boss the chance to kiss and make up with subordinate Phil—a very valuable team member. Remarkably, she chose not to castigate Chad for letting the situation get so out of hand that Phil thought he had to escalate the issue up to her. She realized the achievement-conscious Chad was probably sufficiently mortified by Phil's e-mail. She saw no money in stepping on his neck; and she was right.

This type of brief, clear, and insightful e-mail message has won Lynne the respect of all the division managers. They like having her as a boss because she's patient, allowing them to find their own way. The division heads envy her quiet strength; they watch how she can accomplish a goal, sometimes with nothing more than a nudge or two. She is also very explicit about what displeases her, just as she had been when she reprimanded Chad for using his BlackBerry during her meetings.

Lynne's e-mail tells Chad that she expects him to come to a reasonable resolution with Phil, and then let her know what it is. Politely and with a gentle hand, she has put him on notice to perform. Chad notices the power and leadership Lynne packed into this simple note. He realizes that if he could have composed an e-mail like this, it might have convinced Phil to get the numbers he needed, without a whimper of displeasure from the head of the West Coast group.

Chad is relieved as he checks his calendar for his next appointment. He sees a meeting in the conference room with his management team to go over updates to the Strategic Plan.

10:15 Kim, for Better or for Worse, Leads Mike's Planning Process

Mike has been looking forward to this meeting ever since he saw it in his calendar at home this morning. He even mentioned it to his wife during their morning breakfast ritual. Each day, the two compare notes before taking off in separate directions. Over coffee and cereal they each discuss the most significant part of the upcoming day. Today's choice for the morning sharing session was easy for Mike: He told her about his strategic planning update session. He loves the process of deciding what is most important and how to make it happen. His 10 AM hour is devoted to an update from the strategic planning retreat that was held three months ago.

Every member of his management team is already in the conference room when Mike comes in, right as the meeting is about to start. Once again, he hasn't budgeted his time well. It would have demonstrated stronger leadership for him to be one of the first to arrive, rather than the last. *Oh well, the day's not over yet,* he reasons. Mike measures his leadership performance on the hour, but he never congratulates himself too much for good work or indulges in self-flagellation if he screws up. He sees what works and tries to do it again in the future. When something doesn't work he takes notice, then he quickly lets it go.

The six managers in front of him have their flimsy GBC bound planning workbooks open. It seems to Mike that they are all talking at once. *This is going to be fun,* he thinks, delighted at the energy in the room.

"Okay, Kim, you're running this party," Mike says. "I'm ready when you are." Kim is in charge of production for Mike's division. She's very strong at logistics, but rough around the edges on the communication skills front. His employees complain that she is abrupt and bossy, even though she's usually right. That's why he put her in charge of managing the planning process this year. He felt that both he and the other managers could benefit from watching her organize a large project. He also wanted the opportunity to see her communication skills in action with her peers. It would give him another chance to coach her. He'd been giving her specific direction after watching her in production meetings, but he wanted to see how she handled being in charge of a project when everyone in the room was her political equal.

"Okay people, let's get right to it," Kim begins. "I'm going to start with a review of the tasks that have projected completion dates coming up in the next 60 days, then we'll refresh our memories on the longer-term projects. After I'm done, we'll go down the short-term list, with updates from each of you who are in charge of each task. We'll wind up with hearing from any of you with longer-term tasks who are *off* schedule. We'll all pitch in to help you solve the issue. If everything is progressing well on your task, we'll leave you off the agenda until the next time we meet, in two months."

This is classic Kim, Mike thinks, *at her best and her worst.* It's a great agenda—just the kind he likes. Hit the headlines, tackle what's in front of us first, then discuss longer-term items, but only if they need attention. It's focused, productive, and results-oriented communication. Not only that, this is the second time the group has been prepared by Kim over what they will be working on this morning. A week ago, she sent a brief, bulleted e-mail spelling out what the format of the meeting would be, and she asked for input from everyone on the list. Each manager responded with a line or two about their role, so she knew what was coming. Mike noted how Kim had been preparing herself and the others for the meeting. It was the type of behavior he needed to adopt. He hoped the others also took note of her pattern of organization.

But the "Okay, people" opening was a disaster. Just two words could undermine so much good communication that was to come. Mike has been working to excise these supercilious expressions from Kim's meeting lexicon. He realizes he isn't winning her over yet. She still isn't convinced that "Okay people" will not only hit a lousy note with her direct reports, but it will out-and-out tick off her equals in the room. The introduction would have been much stronger with just the pure and simple, "Let's get to it." He makes a mental note to keep pressure on Kim to dump the patronizing patter.

10:16 Chad Delivers Vague Praise Way Too Early

Chad runs this strategic planning update meeting for the same reason he runs the sales meeting. He's the boss. Bosses lead the meetings —especially important ones like this.

All his managers seated in the big conference room have their heavy strategic planning binders in front of them. Chad has all the detailed notes from his division strategic planning retreat three months earlier, along with the mission and vision statements, SWOT analysis, action items, and assignments bound together in a classy portfolio he picked out himself. He wants this plan to project strength and power. He had lectured that it should stay on top of every manager's desk, for a quick reminder and easy reference for all.

Every one of his managers followed Chad's instructions and kept their binders right next to the phones. Most found they made for elegant coasters.

"Let's start with why we're going through this," Chad says. "I know it's hard to get away from your daily headaches and issues to spend time on strategic planning, but, to be perfectly honest, this is should be considered even more important than the current fires you are now putting out."

Thanks for being perfectly honest, Chad; we all hate it when you lie to us, Jody, the head of sales, thinks to herself. She finds Chad's frequent use of "honestly," "frankly," and "to be perfectly honest," a glaring sign of Chad's weakness as a leader. *Yeah, he's smart; but how smart is he really,* she wonders, *when he keeps repeating disingenuous words that irritate us so much?*

"Remember that strategic thinking is needed to guide and complement tactical actions. We react all day long. Strategic planning gives a chance for us to reflect and figure out our goals and aspirations so we can be the best we can be," Chad says. He's right; but this doesn't do much to set the tone for the meeting.

Now he sounds like an army recruiting ad from the 1980s, Jody sniffs, before shaking herself out of her sarcasm. *Chad's not a bad boss,* she reminds herself, *just completely clueless sometimes.* She turns her attention back to the classy strategic planning portfolio in front of her.

"Okay, Item Number one: our Pacific Rim initiative, which we had agreed we would make a decision on today. Rueben, this was your baby." Chad looks up from the strategic planning notebook and turns to Rueben. "Tell us where stand on this. What have you uncovered?"

Rueben is Chad's Marketing Chief. His task is to study the size of the customer markets and compile important data the group will need to decide whether to invest the time and resources necessary to move forward. About five years ago, they branched out into Western Europe with mixed results. The group—and especially Chad—wants a lot of data from Rueben to help make this a good decision. If they decide to move forward, they will have to prepare a separate business plan with projections and budget to submit to corporate. If not, they'll take it off the table for eight quarters, maybe more. Both EVP Lynne and CFO Andy at corporate have shown a lot of interest in this item.

"Well, I'm starting to feel like we should go to the next level with this one," says Rueben. "My initial research shows, from a demand point, there's no question we should move forward. Here are my figures on the size of the current market, including demographics, broken down by country and the anticipated growth in the next few years, despite the overall economic climate. We look good here."

"Fantastic! Good work, Rueben!" Chad consciously compliments him, with almost a shout to demonstrate his intensity. It's the wrong decision. He pushed the praise button too early, before he had all the information. "Keep going. What else do you have for us?"

"Well, that's the problem," says Rueben. "I'm not done with the competitive analysis yet. I don't know if our current cost structure and price points are going to work. My initial research shows that there are about 15 international players in this space. Unfortunately, with the Meadowvale meltdown, I've only had a chance to study a couple of them. I'm going to need some more time. I'll have all the numbers by our session in the next quarter. I'm really sorry about this, but, to be truthful, we're really lucky I've been able to get anything together for the meeting with everything that's been going on." Rueben is contrite; it's easy to see he does wish that his report was complete. "I hope everyone in the room understands I'm doing absolutely the best I can on this."

Rueben's failure to complete his task on time places Chad in a real leadership bind—when, just a few seconds ago, he went on record praising Rueben for his market analysis. Chad can't shift gears and admonish him so quickly after the praise. That would be inconsistent—one of the key criticisms from his 360 last Friday.

Rueben let the team down by not finishing his work; but he has a good excuse. He rescued the Meadowvale account by jumping in quickly and logging some long hours to resolve a nasty dispute between the sales and production units on this key account. Because of Rueben's quick thinking and dedication, Meadowvale was happy with the last project. In the end, Chad's division had made a decent—though not great—margin on the deal. The dispute initially caused a huge uproar and lots of finger pointing within the division. Now hurt feelings are starting to mend, and Rueben has played a key role in the return to normalcy.

But Chad is embarrassed that he didn't find out until this meeting that Rueben wasn't on schedule with the Pacific Rim report. This analysis had to be completed, regardless of what else was going on in the division. Now Chad will have to explain to Lynne and Andy he was behind on the Asian initiative. He wishes that Rueben, a talented and energetic employee, would have at least given him a heads-up. Together, they probably could have figured out how to get everything done despite the Meadowvale implosion.

It hadn't even occurred to Rueben to let Chad know ahead of time that he wouldn't be able finish his Pacific Rim research assignment. Chad had ordered all hands on deck to rescue the Meadowvale project from disaster; so to Rueben—and everyone else—that meant to put every other task on the back burner. This fire drill had taken everyone off task—not just Rueben. In fact, Chad's weak leadership communication and frequent, overly strident directives causes many managers to go with what would keep him happy at the moment, instead of focusing on the mission of the division. So it seems to everyone, including Chad, that Rueben has performed well under the circumstances. He pitched in and saved a critical customer relationship and important revenue dollars. Chad decides to take an appreciative tone.

"Okay Rueben, I see why you need more time," Chad soft-pedals. "Speaking for myself, and I'm sure everyone in the room, we understand you are doing the best you can, always. We really appreciate your efforts not only on the Meadowvale stuff, but on everything you do for us. That goes without saying."

There's lots of nodding around the room and plenty of encouraging smiles. Chad thinks the positive vibe is good news. But it isn't.

Chad blew a tremendous opportunity here. He took a weak—and easy—position, instead of doing the heavy lifting it takes to be a strong communicator. He should have mildly praised Rueben for the initial work, but also told him and the team that a missed assignment—especially without warning—is hurtful to all. He sent a clear message that missing a deadline is acceptable—as long as you have a good excuse. Chad's acumen with numbers and financial "if/thens" are of little use to him in this critical leadership moment.

10:20 Mike's Team Discovers the Employees Want More

Kim does a nice job of going through all the headlines of the goals that were established three months ago. She turns to Larry, the head of HR.

"Larry, please give us an update on your progress. You committed to providing an in-depth analysis of our employee satisfaction scores. What do you have for us?" Kim asks.

"Well, a few surprises, actually," Larry says. "Let's go over the bullet points. Kim has them on the second page of the booklets." Everyone turns to the right page. Efficiency expert Kim had taken big flip chart pages with all the deliverables from the strategic planning meeting and boiled them down to an efficient little booklet. She and her assistant printed, collated, and bound together the follow-up workbook in the supply room over coffee one morning a few days ago. Mike marvels at how easily Kim cut through a myriad of details and produced just the right package that would help them concentrate on this important meeting.

Larry is the boss of Human Resources for Mike's division. It is a good fit for him to take on the task of providing an analysis of their employee satisfaction scores.

The team's number one goal in the next year is to make sure they have a game plan to attract and keep the best players in the industry, not only nationally, but internationally. Everyone had agreed that the first step should be to find out exactly what current employees like and don't like about the current operation and culture. But the type of information they were seeking called for a series of face-to-face interviews with a wide variety of employees. Larry had put forth the idea in the strategic planning meeting and quickly volunteered to take it on, in addition to his regular workload. It required hours of extra work, but he welcomed the challenge.

"Well, the good news is that we're right on the spot in terms of pay and benefits," Larry explains. "Nobody in the interviews spent a long time on salary issues, even though we gave them plenty of openings. We're regarded as reasonable and fair with our employee compensation, according to our people and what they hear from their friends at other companies. Some of the newer competitors pay more than we do. But they don't have the track record we do, or the corporate support that we have being one division of a larger company."

"Is that why I don't see any recommendations in terms of compensation?" Kim asks. *Boy, Kim is good,* Mike thinks. *She put two and two together faster than anyone else in the room.*

"That's right. We don't need to look at making any changes there. Pay is not an issue for us; we're right where we should be. But I do want us to consider investing more in training, based on some of the surprising things we heard in the interviews."

This catches everyone off guard in the room, except for Kim, Mike, and, of course, Larry. The others are surprised because Mike's division already provides a ton of training for the entire staff at all levels. And the management decided they'd do a lot more than just *provide* continuous training for every employee; a year ago they had required 24 hours per year of approved continuing education or critical skill set training for every employee.

In fact, Larry made the 24-hour requirement an important part of every employee's yearly review format.

"The training requirement that we were concerned about everyone being able to handle with their hectic schedules, apparently isn't enough," Larry explains. "They want more." No one in management had anticipated this.

This is a delightful bit of news. The training mandate had come with the caveat that every employee was still responsible for all of their normal responsibilities, even with 24 hours—3 full workdays—lopped out of the year. You couldn't miss a deadline just because you had a training class. You had to make it work, one way or another.

"How much more do they want?" Louis, the sales manager, asks.

"Well, this is going to floor you," Larry answers, with a smile. "More than three quarters of the people we sat down say they want it upped to 48 hours." The managers look at each other; the room is still for a moment. Kim and Mike already know about the requests for more training because they wound up helping Larry with the interviews. About a month after the strategic planning meeting, Larry had asked for Kim's advice on his employee interview deliverable. He told her he was worried he wouldn't be able to complete it on time for the update meeting. "The Palmer termination may take a lot more of my time than we anticipated," Larry said. "Looks like he and his attorney want to go to the mat on this one. Depositions may start as early as next week."

Like all the managers, Kim knew that Palmer firing thing might turn out like this. The legal process was starting to heat up, and that meant Larry would lose huge blocks of his schedule over the next three months.

He went on. "But I'm still in a big jam on these employee one-on-ones from the strategic planning session. Doing these in-depth interviews is critical to finding out what powers our 'Sat' scores."

"Okay, I think I remember we agreed on 30 interviews during the planning meeting. How many do you think you can get through in time?" Kim asked.

"I can make it through more than half. I can do 20 of them," Larry said. "But I'm going to need help with the other 10. I won't be able to touch them with all the legal stuff going on."

"Okay, Larry, let me think on this for a few days," Kim said.

By the end of the week, Kim had approached him with a solution. Kim would take six of the interviews off his plate, while Mike had agreed to do the last four. That would give Larry the 30 interviews he needed to find out what the employees really wanted out of the division.

Now, two months later, the management team is right on track to take action on Larry's important findings. With little debate, they decide to meet the employees' ambitious request halfway by increasing the mandatory training and continuing education requirement to 36 hours. Ellen says she can find the budget dollars for the outside trainers and classes, if the other managers can give up their employees' time and still stay productive.

Everyone is on board, and Mike signs off on it, saying the new training hours mandate will be effective starting day one of the next fiscal year. Over the last year, he has pounced on every one of his managers when they missed a deadline to which they had agreed; and he wasn't reticent about doing it in front of others.

"When you miss a deadline, it tells all of us you didn't think you had to do what you said you would," Mike would fume. "If you need help, ask for help loudly and early, long before the deadline. We will pitch in as a team and help you out—every time! I promise that you'll get the help you need. If you still can't make the deadline, at least we'll know it ahead of time. And we can make adjustments."

He would always end with the same direct and powerful statement: "Any missed deadlines had better be because of some type of serious family emergency. Otherwise, I'll know you don't think you have to do what you say you will do; and that is you telling us not to trust you."

So when Larry first sensed that the Palmer case was going to gobble up his time, he knew just what to do. He went straight to Kim, the boss of the strategic planning process, and he found he even didn't even need to ask for help. Kim beat him to the punch. She immediately gave Larry the help he needed by rolling up her sleeves and taking on a burden of the task. When Mike heard about the jam Larry was in, he gladly took four of the interviews from Kim. Mike's team had accomplished the first task they had taken on as a part of the strategic planning process. It all worked out so well because Larry knew he could and had to ask for help to get his job done.

Larry's report energizes the room. Six of the next seven managers follow suit, delivering valuable information and reports that provide the baseline for the managers to make decisions and formulate the next step of actions. During the headline portion at the meeting's beginning, Kim had let everyone know that one of the managers was running late on one task. But she and Mike had known about it for more than a month; the three of them had already figured out how to get back on track. The rest of the team volunteered some helpful ideas and short cuts as well in an attempt to help the manager get caught up on the task in time for the group's next quarterly meeting.

Mike is pleased as the meeting breaks up, and he takes a few minutes to praise Kim for a number of specific successes she fostered. He also tells her no more "Okay people" remarks. She smiles, admits it was over-the-top "bossy," and then reminds Mike that she is still a "work in progress." He agrees and says he'll keep coaching her.

10:45 Hits and Misses for Chad's Team

Rueben's Pacific Rim report set the stage for the rest of the strategic planning update. Chad's management team had committed to completing six tasks by this date; but only two of them have been wrapped up as promised. The other four are in various stages of development and aren't quite ready for next steps. Just like Reuben, the champions of each one of the tasks has made significant headway, but they finished far short of completion. And, like Rueben, they all have compelling excuses.

Chad feels that since he let Rueben's failure go without correction, he can't do much to show frustration or displeasure with the others. He starts to feel the same irritation he experienced at the dry cleaners early in the morning. But now he is experiencing a different reaction. Three hours after complaining about the woman at the dry cleaners to his wife, he is becoming more introspective.

He does have strong people on his team, ones who care about the operation. Rueben's efforts are a great example. *We're not getting the job done, and maybe it's me, not them*, he thinks.

10:00 AM

Don't Be That Boss Lessons

10:01 Lynne Gives Chad Some Breathing Room

✓ To learn how to improve your own communication skills, study the winning ways of others.

10:15 Kim, for Better or for Worse, Leads Mike's Planning Process

✓ Evaluate your employees' communication skills in every meeting that they lead, and look for ways to encourage positive results. Take the time to point out negative words and expressions.

10:16 Chad Delivers Vague Praise Way Too Early

✓ The best bosses praise infrequently, but they do so with tremendous impact. Praising too early—before you have sufficient information—will likely make you look foolish.

10:20 Mike's Team Discovers the Employees Want More

✓ Encourage all of the team to communicate all the time about wins, misses, hiccups, and near-disasters.

(continued)

(*continued*)

10:45 Hits and Misses for Chad's Team

✓ Tying the success of your own communication skills to your teams' performance is a critical step to becoming a better boss.

11:00 AM Customer Standoff:

Accept Real Blame but Never Fall on Your Sword

11:05 Mike Readies Louis for Combat

Mike barely has time to hit the restroom and then refill his coffee cup in the break room before Louis flags him down in the hallway.

"We've got Denise Sizemore in 10 minutes, you know," Louis warns. "I hope you remember we're not in good shape on this one."

"Yes, not only do I remember, but I'm looking forward to it in a weird kind of way," Mike says. "Yesterday I looked over

75

the e-mail trails between you two over the last few weeks. Not a pretty sight." Mike is actually ahead of the game for the first time today.

"Well, you're right on that . . . it's ugly," Louis says. "But why on earth would you say that you're looking forward to it? That's like saying you can't wait for your next colonoscopy."

Mike laughs. Louis is right; the meeting with Denise won't be a ton of fun. But Mike still has his reasons for his anticipation. "Well, for one, I'm looking forward to seeing you in action. Last week we prepared well for this," Mike explains. "Second, I'm interested in her reaction. She does a damn good job of negotiating for her company, so I want to see how she responds."

"So you're not expecting a world war?" Louis asks.

"No way," Mike says. "I'm guessing she'll back off as soon as you go forward with your plan. But she'll still try to get more than what's fair from us. That's what will make this interesting."

11:07 Chad Comes Up with "The Perfect Storm" Tactic

Chad and Jody have been huddling together in Chad's office since the planning session broke up minutes earlier. One of their biggest customers, Steve Moreno, had requested a face-to-face with them to discuss the delivery of his last two orders—both of which had been late.

Steve gave Jody a sarcastic answer last week as they were scheduling the meeting over the phone: "No, no, no. I'm more than happy to drive all the way across town and come to your office. I wouldn't want you to get lost along the way and show up late," he had told her.

"Do we have anywhere to go on this, or are we totally up against the wall?" Chad asks Jody.

"I don't know what to say to him. We screwed up, big-time, on his last two orders. I'd be pissed, too," Jody offers.

"Okay, here's how we'll play it. We'll say we're sorry and all that, but he has to realize it was a weird set of circumstances that caused the late shipments . . . you know, 'the perfect storm' thing, which is totally true," Chad says. "You take the lead, and I'll jump in when needed."

"Sounds like a plan," Jody shrugs. She doesn't think it's a very solid plan. Steve Moreno is a long-term customer. He's a reasonable guy; but he isn't a pushover. She's worried it's going to be rougher sledding than Chad is preparing for.

"Okay, let's you and I show a united front, and hope for the best," Chad says as he stands up straight and grabs his BlackBerry and his notes.

11:15 Louis Takes the Early Hit

Louis, Mike, and Denise trade some minor pleasantries over the traditional guest "coffee, water, or soda?" ritual. Louis marvels at Mike's demeanor with Denise. He's friendly, but not gratuitous. He asks meaningful questions about Denise's company and her kids, but nothing that smacks of brownnosing. To anyone unfamiliar with the reason for the visit, it looks like Mike is doing a great job of naturally connecting to a valuable customer, with no agenda in mind.

Denise, in turn, is professional with Louis and Mike. She doesn't cop an attitude or act snippy. That doesn't mean she won't once they got going, but at least they're off to a good start. Louis takes note of Mike's steady performance early on in what is going to be a trying meeting. Mike isn't sweating, nor is he coming on too strong. He's just pleasant, with a nice touch of confidence.

Without any prompting from Mike, Louis officially starts the meeting.

"Look, Denise. We know we've been out of sync with you from day one on your last order, and the purpose of this meeting is to make it right," Louis says.

Denise leans forward and clasps her hands across the conference table from Louis and Mike.

"Okay, that's a good start," says Denise. "As long as you realize you're the ones who are out of sync with me, not the other way around."

"Yes, that's how we see it as well, Denise," says Louis. "This is our issue, not yours. But right now I want Mike to hear firsthand from you what went wrong. Please go over what happened, so when we start anew, we'll be working from the same template."

"Great. This is a nice touch with you being here, Mike. I'm impressed." Denise says. "But it might hurt some along the way, ripping off the Band-Aid all at once. Your team hasn't performed very well. And I didn't even stick it to Louis's guys very hard during the pricing negotiations. Looking back, I probably should have. This has been a real pain in the rear ever since I gave this project to you."

Louis notices Mike was right about Denise's plan. She complimented Mike first and then wound up to deliver a major haircut.

"I know," says Mike, "and that's why I'm all ears. Louis and I want to hear everything you have to say, now that we're together."

Louis and Denise then proceed with the blow by blow of the contract foul-ups.

The legal paperwork Denise received from the division didn't match the proposal she had approved from Louis and other members of the sales team. This wasn't some casual phone chat about a minor order; the meetings had taken place over several weeks.

There were a number of different menu items and services in the contract she did not agree to or want.

Several items she had stressed that she needed more than once—and were fully outlined in the proposal—were nowhere to be seen in the contract. "Do your lawyers know how to 'cut and paste' in Word?" she asked. "It's really easy; my seventh grader does it all the time in his book reports."

The final price on the contract is now so screwy with things she didn't want included and things she needed omitted that she can't figure out what she owes. But whatever the price is, she claims that it's way too much.

"If you guys struggle so much just getting the paperwork right, I'm scared about what on earth will happen once your engineers have to start doing real work, which is already behind schedule," Denise says as she leans back in her chair. She pauses for a minute, looks hard, and continues. "We also have begun to wonder over at our place about some of the other stuff in progress we have going with you guys, based on this contract debacle."

Denise's company had hired Mike's division for two other projects that are in various stages of completion. It would be very disruptive to Denise's operation to pull the plug on Mike's guys and find another vendor. So this last jab is nothing more than a toothless threat. But she is good. It sure sounded like she meant it, especially since she has every right to follow through on her words. The contract she received was a mess.

Mike doesn't flinch from the "take my toys and go home" line because he's well prepared for it. His words of caution just before the meeting let Louis know that Denise would beat on them pretty hard. And, right on cue, she had.

Louis waits for Denise to finish. Even though she piles it on, taking a few liberties with the facts, she gets most of it right. She clasps her hands again and looks at Louis and Mike. Louis starts in.

"Denise, this was sloppy, sloppy work on our end. It's our fault and mine in particular as the sales manager. I didn't check the contracts before they went out the door to you, and I didn't respond quickly enough after your first e-mail. I'm sorry that we did a lousy job for you. We're very happy you are doing business with us, and we are glad you are a customer of ours—both now, and hopefully going forward. We know you have other choices; we always want to be the first choice. This was not a good way of demonstrating that to you."

"Well, when you're right, you're right, Louis. But what the hell happened here? You guys are usually better than this, much better," Denise says.

"Well, I could go through all the gory details with you, but they're boring and embarrassing," Louis explained. "Besides, we don't think you should have to be worried or even care about why we don't have our act together. Here's what's important: We let you down and now we're going to make it right."

Denise laughs, "You're right! I really don't care what happened. All I want is for you guys to stop giving me a headache.

My head may stop hurting after you explain what you meant by 'make it right.' *Now* you have my full attention."

11:16 The Customer's Not Buying What Chad and Jody Are Selling

Chad, Jody, and Steve Moreno go through a stiff round of small talk while they get seated. Steve is not very talkative and obviously wants to get this show on the road.

"Well, Steve, we certainly appreciate your coming over here to meet with us," Chad says. "Jody has filled me on what's been going on with your orders and we're here to explain to you what happened and how we have things under control now."

"Oh, I know what happened," Steve jumps in. "What happened is you were late with my orders. It was five days late the first time, and seven days late with the next one. I didn't make the trip to find out what happened." He's getting heated. This isn't an act. "I know that you didn't deliver when you said you would, not once, but twice. So, I'm well aware of what happened. My question is, what are you going to do about it?"

Steve's tone is harsh and direct. He doesn't want to chat about circumstances on their end. He is putting them on notice, but he wants to get something out of this meeting with Chad and Jody other than just tales of woe. Chad sticks to the game plan.

"We'll get to that for sure, Steve," Chad says. "But first, Jody has to explain what happened from our end. It was really an unfortunate set of circumstances, which we want you to understand. Being late with deliveries is not how we do business. That's why we're happy for the chance to meet with you face-to-face. Go ahead, Jody."

Steve manages to turn and look at Jody, ready for her explanation; only it isn't with anticipation. He looks bored and angry.

"Well, it was really a mixture of three crazy things colliding all at once. Your orders hit our system right as our IT guys were finishing off the yearly upgrade to our shipping software. In the mix, your orders didn't make the transfer over to the new database. This was the first bit of lousy luck." Jody is making a brave case. Steve nods slightly, but he isn't agreeing.

"Here's where it gets worse. Our warehouse assistant manager, who always catches software issues like this stuff when she goes through the manual paperwork, is on maternity leave for another two weeks. The temp agency sent us someone who really left a lot to be desired, so we have to deal with training a new temp right in the middle of the software changeover." Chad can sense Jody losing steam some as she explains it all. He's right; it isn't convincing.

"Finally, your purchase order came though on the 30th of the month, which is always the craziest day of the month around here. I'm sure you can relate to that with your customers." Jody holds her out her hands slightly, with the gentle palms-up movement, and cocks her head to the side, "If this had happened on the 20th or even the 25th, probably someone along the way would have caught it for sure."

"So you can see, Steve," Jody prepares for this big finish, "it was just 'the perfect storm.' We hate to disappoint you, but it was just bizarre timing of three pieces of bad luck that led to the late shipments. Nothing more, nothing less."

Nice recovery, Jody, thinks Chad. And the perfect storm thing sounded pretty doggone convincing as Jody explained it. Maybe they'd get out of this without too much collateral damage.

But Chad isn't ready for the whack to the back of the head that's coming.

"That is the perfect storm, alright," Steve begins, with zero sympathy in his voice. "But I think you have me confused with someone who gives a damn. You guys were late—twice in two weeks—and that left me sucking wind with my customers on their critical orders. On top of that, I got no warning from you. Your software problems, a new baby for one of your employees, and an order on the last day of the month are immaterial to me."

Chad decides to push back. "Don't you think you're being a little hard on us, Steve?" Chad asks without much conviction. "I mean, that was a whole lot of lousy karma in one week for us, wasn't it?"

"Look Chad," Steve says, "You guys have done a pretty good job for us over the years, which is why I'm over here right now, wasting a morning. But I didn't lose two hours of my life with the drive across town to get a lame bit of education on lousy karma, perfect storms, or the miracle of childbirth. They are all just excuses. I got screwed on this. Big-time. That's what happened."

Chad gulps. Jody flushes. This is bad.

"And let me tell you something in case you don't know it. Your financial department doesn't give a red rat's petunia about my perfect storms when it comes to your invoices. I get a nasty warning letter at 35 days and then you guys cut me off 50 days until I'm current. My employees have babies, too; but I'd sure better get my precious little check out to your crack AR team or I'm toast. Can't you see that's why I'm losing it here? What's good for the goose apparently is not good for the gander." Steve exhales deeply.

Steve spat out a lot in the last few sentences. And, despite the vitriol, it is a powerful argument. Chad's division, in keeping with company orders, does keep a tight credit rein on all customers.

"Okay, Steve, I get it," Chad says. He looks uncomfortable for a moment. Then he decides, without warning Jody, to cave—fast and hard. "I think you're going to like what I'm going to come up with for you."

Steve nods; and Jody begins to worry. Chad usually costs the division money when he wings it in his discussions like these.

11:36 Denise Asks for More Than Louis Offers

"We apologize for this mess, Denise, and we want you to know that we take full responsibility for it," Louis continues, without prompting from Mike. "So here's what we're going to do. I hope you'll forgive us and we can move forward."

Louis follows up with a detailed explanation of how he plans to spend the next three hours creating a new, correct contract that matches the proposal. He'll have it couriered over to Denise's office by 4:45 PM. He adds that he will cut the price of the project by 7 percent without eliminating a single menu item from the proposal Denise had approved.

"We need to take this hit on this, Denise, to show you we're serious," Louis says. "I know we can't make up for your time or frustration; but we have to give up some margin on this to show you we get it. You'll do well on this deal with the 7 percent drop in price this time. We want you to be happy and know that, when we screw up, we will make it right."

"Okay guys. This shows me you're sorry. I like the price cut, and I'll be in my office waiting for your courier, Louis, just before 5 PM. Just make sure the contract is perfect, and we'll sign it tomorrow. We need to get moving on this," Denise smiles. But she isn't done yet.

"Can you please call off the dogs in the accounting department? We get these calls from your AR guys at just 35 days on an invoice. You can almost set a timer to it," Denise explains. "Look, we've be doing business together for a while. We try to pay at 30 days, but sometimes that's just not possible, given everything that's going on," she says. Then Denise makes "the ask" and it is a big one.

"How about we change our terms to 45 days going forward, and we'll work really hard from our end to make sure, at the latest, we're getting you paid at 60 days, which I'm sure won't happen very often. This will make our good relationship even stronger." Denise isn't kidding with this; it's a serious request.

After a beat or two of silence, Mike is ready to speak; but Louis beats him to it. "That's not going to work for us, Denise, and let me tell you why," Louis says. He's not defensive; but he demonstrates conviction. Even though he's just apologized and cut the price for this particular project, he stands his ground. Andy, the company's CFO, based all of his projections and financial models on customers paying on a 30-day net, with some allowances for the occasional payment that went beyond 45 days from good customers. But even good customers didn't have much leeway. Steady, consistent cash flow was the bedrock behind the ability of all the divisions to provide great value to customers and timely payment to vendors. Lynne and the rest of the management team of the company backed Andy strongly on this issue, and all the division managers had their marching orders: Discount the price every now and then if you must, but stick to a 30-day net payment to maintain cash flow.

"The success of our division and our whole company depends on us maintaining 30-day terms with all of our customers—even great ones like you, Denise. We're not going to be able to move on that for you." Louis stops talking. It is Denise's turn.

"Hey Mike, can you help me out on this one here?" Denise presses slightly, but with a lot of skill. "Sounds like Louis here had too much of the company Kool-Aid this morning. Can you get him to agree to relax the 30-day rule some? I'd really appreciate it." Denise is a great negotiator. Even though she is going over Louis's head right in front of him, she does it with charm and humor, which makes the second request sound reasonable. There's no tension in the room.

"I can't help out, for two reasons, Denise. First, Louis is calling the shots here. I'm just here to observe and learn something from both of you," Mike says. "And the second point won't be what you want to hear, either. I drank the same Kool-Aid as Louis. We all do every day." Mike smiles, "We have to stick with 30 days. There's no flexibility at all on this item."

"Okay, I get it," Denise says, "but will you do me at least one favor in the meantime? Mike, will you please ask the big bosses down the hall to give just us a break on this going forward? I promise I won't tell anyone else about it, and it would make me look really great to my boss." Denise flashes a Dentyne-like smile, showing all the choppers. But she isn't kidding. She's still pushing.

Mike admires her and thinks she'd make a great addition to anyone's team.

"Denise, despite your formidable skills of persuasion, I'm not even going to ask for you," Mike says. "It won't work with the CFO, and it won't help either one of us."

"Really?" She asks slowly, just trying one last time.

"Yes, really, Denise; but boy, you are good," Mike answers.

"You're right, I am good." Denise says. She stands up with a burst of energy and another big smile.

"Louis, why don't you come by yourself with the contracts at the end of the day, instead of sending the couriers? I'll even make sure there's a fresh pot of coffee going in case you want to stick around a bit to talk about some other ideas we've been tossing around for next quarter. Mike, you lay off the Kool-Aid. You boys are too well trained."

11:42 Chad Overplays the Apology Card

Chad turns to Jody and makes a pronouncement with a slow and deliberate tone. "For the rest of the year, Jody, starting today, we're going to provide a 5 percent across the board discount on all of Steve's orders. That's on top of the sharp pencil we always use for him. Jody, can you make sure the rest of the sales team knows of the special Steve Moreno discount?"

"Yes, I will, Chad." She takes out her BlackBerry, "I'll create an agenda item right now for our sales meeting next Monday. We'll make sure everyone knows." Jody is sharp, backing up Chad without a fight.

She makes a mental note to tell Louis—her counterpart in Mike's organization—that she resisted the urge to pull a "Sonny Corleone," despite the fact she lost three-eighths of her tongue while biting through it. Louis would get the *Godfather* reference immediately and know she had wanted to disagree with Chad, but she had the good sense to "never show her true feelings to outsiders."

She had a feeling Chad would pull a stunt like this once Steve bared his teeth. But she also knew that Chad didn't have to go this far. The "perfect storm" idea was weak, and once it had failed to soften Steve, Chad was overcompensating with this year-long discount. If they had discussed this ahead of time in greater detail, she would have kept him from making such a drastic concession. Steve probably would have been placated with a 5 percent discount on each of the screwed up orders. If Chad wanted to be a real mensch about it, he might have gone to 7 percent—but *just* on these two orders. Giving Steve a permanent discount for the year will screw up their margins and give them less wiggle room with other customers as the year goes on. Also, it will be hell to get Steve back to his original price once he gets used to the discount.

As for Steve, he is surprised at the 5 percent year-long discount, but he has the moxie not to show it. And Jody is right; he would have been delighted with a real apology and a small price cut of the two late orders. Instead, he got a pile of dumb excuses, and that made him hot.

He's surprised that Chad, buttoned down and sharp as a tack when it comes to numbers, folded so quickly instead of just admitting he didn't have his operational act together. That alone probably would have cooled Steve down. Instead, Steve decides to keep Chad on the run. Maybe there's more money in it.

"Okay, I'll accept your apology; and I'm looking forward to the discount. But, while we're at it, can we look at one more item that would really help me to forget the mess you've got in your shipping department?" Steve asks.

Chad thinks this is a good sign, "Yes, of course. What else can we do for you?"

"Can we get your financial guys to relax their terms a little?" Steve asks. "Not a lot, just a little. If we could go net 45 on our orders to the end of the year along with that great discount you've offered, why, it would be like those two late shipments never even happened, as far as I'm concerned."

Jody looks at Chad, hoping he will come clean and say they right thing to Steve. She is disappointed.

"Steve, I'm going to do everything I can to get our credit guys to offer 45-day terms. It's a reasonable request, after all, given all that's going on. I'm making no promises, because our rules on terms are handed down on tablets from corporate; but I certainly can try. Can I get back to you next week on this?"

"Sure, that would be great," says Steve. "Next order on time though, with the 5 percent discount, we're all clear on that right?"

"You bet," says Chad.

"Well, then this morning wasn't a waste of time after all," says Steve, as he is leaving.

After he walks out of the office, Chad says to Jody, "Whew, that was brutal, but I guess it wound up okay, don't you think?"

"Yeah, it was okay I guess in the end; and yeah, it was brutal," Jody says. *The year-long discount isn't a complete disaster*, she thinks, *if that's how Chad wants to evaluate things*. What *isn't* okay with her is that Chad knew he had no chance of changing the payment terms for Steve. Oh, he didn't out-and-out lie about it; Chad, being Chad, absolutely will do what he said and will follow up. He'll weakly ask Andy, the corporate CFO, to make an exception for this customer. But Andy won't budge and Chad knew it, ahead of time. Andy will probably wonder why Chad would even ask about relaxing the terms.

Jody doesn't respect Chad's weak qualifying choice of words like "I can certainly try." Chad knew even before he said it that he would be calling Steve back with disappointing news on the terms next week. He was placating Steve Moreno, instead of treating him like a trusted business colleague. Jody would have actually looked up to Chad if he could have just told Steve straight up that they'd have to stick with 30-day terms. The meeting still would have ended on an upbeat note.

It's turning out to be a rough morning for Jody. Chad isn't a very motivating boss, she's starting to realize. If times were better, she'd get an updated resume out on the street. Instead, she decides to just try to keep her head down, deal with Chad, and get through this part of her career. Maybe she'll update her resume tonight as well.

11:00 AM

Don't Be That Boss Lessons

11:05 Mike Readies Louis for Combat

✓ Make certain that you and your employees are prepared for every in-person customer meeting, including what is likely to happen, as well as discussing contingencies for what could go wrong.

(continued)

(continued)

11:07 Chad Comes Up with "The Perfect Storm" Tactic

✓ Don't offer customers reasons why you and your team have not delivered. They don't care. They just want to know when and how the issue will be taken care of.

11:15 Louis Takes the Early Hit

✓ Strong admissions of failure without excuses are a critical part of powerful leadership communication.

11:16 The Customer's Not Buying What Chad and Jody Are Selling

✓ Excuses for failure only make a bad communication scenario even worse.

11:36 Denise Asks for More Than Louis Offers

✓ Teach your employees not to give away the store, even when admitting a mistake. Make sure they know the makeup offer fits the magnitudes of the miscue.

11:42 Chad Overplays the Apology Card

✓ When you prepare poorly for a customer meeting, you wind up giving away margin you don't have to.

12:00 PM

Chad Negotiates When Mike Doesn't Have To

12:01 Chad Offers an Olive Branch

After the Steve Moreno meeting, Chad spends 10 minutes in his office going over all the variables in the mess with Phil. He's having a difficult time grappling with why things had revved up and got out of control so quickly. He decides to make a bold move, the type he doesn't usually take. He picks up the phone and dials Phil's number.

"Chad, I told you in my e-mail that I wouldn't have the numbers to you until at least a half an hour from now," Phil answers the phone without even saying hello. He had debated even picking it up when he saw it was Chad.

"I know that, Phil." Chad says. "I want to talk to you about our e-mails this morning."

"Okay, I have something to say about them, too," Phil says. "But you called; you go first."

"Well, I want to say I'm sorry for the tough words and nasty tone in my early e-mail this morning," Chad says. "While I sure needed the numbers, I shouldn't have come on so strong."

Phil is caught off guard. It isn't like Chad to come clean so quickly. Phil wonders if Lynne is behind this bit of surprising contrition. *Maybe,* he figures; *but if so, it would have taken a different form.* If Chad was responding to a direct command from Lynne, he would have sent Phil a formal e-mail of apology that could be documented. Chad loves to document his actions.

No, this is Chad doing the right thing. *Unusual,* Phil thinks; but he isn't going to question it. Phil decides to keep the good karma flowing and not push back—even though he is still irritated about Chad's morning e-mail.

"Well, I appreciate the call, Chad. That means a lot to me," Phil says. "I was pretty torqued when I got your e-mail. I honestly didn't know you needed the numbers this morning."

Chad is faced with a major decision. He can keep the integrity of this apologetic phone call intact, or he can switch gears and start reminding Phil exactly when he made a commitment about the projected purchases from the vendor. Boy, this is a tough call. He decides to take another chance.

"I understand Phil, but the reason for this call isn't to go over that. I need to let you know I came on way too strong in my e-mail. I reread it a couple of minutes ago, and I now regret sending it. I should have just picked up the phone and we could have had this thing figured out in a couple of minutes. Get the numbers to me when you can, and I'll take care of everything from my end." *There, I did it,* thinks Chad. *No "yeah I know, but."*

This feels weird, thinks Chad. He knew as soon as he apologized that he was not simply pandering to Phil. But it does feel strange to own up to his mistake without the quid pro quo of getting a concession from the other guy, who, let's face it, had wronged him as well. He lets Phil off the hook, not to curry his favor, but because Chad's apology takes necessary precedence for his egregious e-mail. Chad knows his actions were far more hurtful to the company's performance than Phil's missed morning deadline.

On the other end of the call, Phil is positive now that a directive from Lynne isn't lurking in background. If Chad were just covering his rear he would have used semi-apologetic phrases like "I'm sorry if you think I came on too strong." Instead, his apology is too direct, with no qualifiers. *Wow,* thinks Phil, *this is a new Chad.*

"Well, while we're owning up to mistakes Chad, I probably shouldn't have CC'd Lynne in my response to you. That was pretty crappy on my part, but boy I was mad, especially first thing Monday morning. I'm sorry about that. I'd take it back if I could," Phil says. "Hope you're not in too much hot water over this."

"Well, it got Lynne's attention, but she's going to let us figure it out," Chad says. "I got to hand it to you, though, pretty daring to CC her directly on this so I could see it. You didn't play any games, which I respect." Chad isn't just playing nice.

"Yeah, well, now I feel silly about it," admits Phil. "It makes us both look kinda weak and downright pissy to her."

"You're right, it does," says Chad. "We'll here's what I'm going to do from now on. When I'm up against the wall on something I need your help on, I'm going to pick up the phone instead of blasting off an e-mail to you. Only I'll never call before 6 AM your time, I promise. Listen, I've got to run off to a lunch appointment with somebody we're trying to hire. I hope you have a good rest of the day."

"Hey, Chad, there's just one more thing before you go." Phil says.

Now that Chad has taken a strong leadership initiative, Phil decides to make Chad's vendor dilemma his major focus immediately. Phil still has other pressing tasks on his desk in front of him, but he'll work around them.

"Chad, do you have just a second to send me your vendor purchasing projections right now, before you leave the office?"

Phil offers to bring in an additional staff member and immediately crunch their West Coast numbers for the next year, add them to the report, then reformat the document and get the report back to Chad by 12:45, eastern time.

"Yeah, um, that would be great, Phil. I'll get it off to your right now," Chad says.

"Okay, you'll have a full report for the vendor when you show up at his door. Make sure you show him who the frickin' boss is, and get those price breaks we need. I'll be rooting for you here."

"I will, Phil. Hey, I'm glad I picked up the phone and called you," Chad says.

"Yeah, me too," says Phil.

Chad puts down the phone and then e-mails the file for Phil to complete. *Boy, I didn't see that coming,* he thinks to himself as he heads out the door to lunch.

12:06 Mike Finds the Shoe on the Other Foot

Mike sits at the neighborhood bistro, waiting for his new prospective employee. He doesn't pick a trendy or expensive spot, but, rather, a comfortable, converted four-bedroom bungalow with great daily specials. It is run by a married couple, and Mike has been coming here for years with his wife. He likes the comfortable atmosphere and the menu, which features Pacific Rim and American classic food. He makes it a habit to take final interview candidates here to seal the deal. His new prospective hire is late, but at least she called to give him a heads-up.

"I'm so sorry," Colleen said on the phone. "This is the last lunch I wanted to be late to. I just couldn't get out of the meeting I was in. Are we still on?"

"Sure, of course. Please take your time," Mike said. "I run late all the time, too. Relax, we'll be fine." That last part isn't really true. He has that vendor negotiation scheduled for 1:15. He'll have to call now to them to let them know he is running late. Not helpful.

Mike finds himself slightly irritated at Colleen. He doesn't give her any attitude because he wants a pleasant lunch meeting when he makes the formal ask for her to join his team. But she is messing up his afternoon.

Then Mike actually chuckles out loud. *That's a case of the pot calling the kettle black,* he thinks. He is constantly late and often makes matters worse by leaving important documents behind. He realizes, *well, this is what it feels like to be on the other end of it.*

He gets out his BlackBerry and pulls up the notes menu. He had e-mailed his friend Chad over the weekend to ask him if he knew of any time-management coaches who had a good reputation. Everyone in the company turned to Chad as the expert repository of information about executive learning, coaches, and continuous education resources. Chad e-mailed Mike back within 10 minutes, giving him three contacts, complete with websites. Mike cut and pasted the information into the notes view of Outlook so he could take advantage of a moment like this.

With Colleen running late, Mike takes the opportunity to call one of the coaches and is lucky enough to find her at her desk. Quickly, he sets an initial appointment. He likes the approach she outlines to him over the phone. He pounds out a quick e-mail to Chad, thanking him for the reference and telling him the first coach on his list is quite impressive. *Wow, I can make better use of my time when I put my mind to it,* he congratulates himself.

He also makes a quick call to his supplier, who he was scheduled to meet right after lunch. He gets Gregg's voice mail: *Gregg, this is Mike. I am looking forward to our meeting after lunch. I'm running late right now and wanted to know if you could give me 15 minutes of leeway. I'll try to make up the time over my lunch meeting, but I'm not confident I will be able to. See you at 1:30, and I apologize for the inconvenience.*

Colleen walks in the restaurant. He rises to shake her hand and get the lunch started.

12:15 Chad Makes His Case

Chad and his new prospective hire go through a gentle round of small talk in the downtown club over iced tea. This is Chad's favorite choice for final interviews and employee promotions. Chad likes the long elevator ride up to the top of the downtown tower, and he feels it makes a strong impression to interview candidates as well. *The spectacular view of the city adds impact to every meeting,* he reasons.

The waiter in a black bow tie and white linen coat, engraved with the club name above the breast pocket, brings the meals. Chad starts his pitch. He had been going over what he would say in the car ride over and felt he was prepared to make a successful offer.

"James, we're the right company for you right now and perhaps for a long time going forward. Let me tell you why." Chad congratulates himself for making a straightforward, nonflowery opening. He had toyed with several other intros to the hiring discussion and then thought of what he would want to hear. He's glad he decided to lead with the headline.

James nods his head vigorously while chewing, letting Chad know this is off to a good start.

"Well, let's review where our division is in the marketplace and where you are in your career path for a few minutes. This will show us we are a good fit," says Chad.

Chad makes a strong argument. While his division isn't racking up big growth numbers, they are holding their own in a tough market. Chad has the budget to add three key employees this year, and James will play a critical role in helping the division improve its revenue and service offerings.

There is more nodding from James and a quick smile or two between bites.

So far, very good, Chad thinks. Now comes the fun part. He's ready to make the offer, get James on board, and save the company some money in the process. Chad has prepared well for this. First, he asked his HR manager to give him a detailed market salary report for the position he was offering James. With that information in hand, he spent an evening on the Internet doing more salary and qualification research. Finally, he reached out to some friends from B-school who worked at large companies with access to even broader databases than he and his HR director had. He calculated late last night what he would offer James and how far he would go in the negotiation.

"James, we want you to come to work for us, right away. I'm happy that, despite all the economic turmoil, we're moving forward with our company and we want strong players like you. That's why I'm pleased to offer you the position we've been discussing at a salary of $73,000 a year. We hope you'll accept."

It's a low-ball offer. Not an insulting offer, but at the low end of the scale. In some companies, people like James are making as much as $85,000. James is well qualified for this job. Despite the economic climate, he has a strong enough skill set that is still in demand. There is a good chance he's fielding other offers. That's why Chad has done so much homework. He wants to be ready to punch and counterpunch on salary with James and get this guy on board quickly without giving away too much.

This opening low number salvo is a calculated move on Chad's part. He knows James likes the direction of his division and the company overall. He will have good opportunities in the years ahead. That makes it a great fit for both of them. The $73,000 is a reasonable but not great offer. Chad is satisfied. And he's ready for the battle ahead. He knows James will counter.

"Chad, that is a reasonable offer, and I'm flattered you've asked me to join your team," James says. "But, from my perspective, I'm disappointed in the $73,000 salary that's on the table. Are you receptive to discussing it?"

"Well, I don't know how much wiggle room I'm really going to have on this one, what with the economy and all," Chad says, "but please tell me what's on your mind." Chad isn't telling the truth. He knows exactly how much wiggle room he has.

12:20 Mike Paints His Picture of the Future for Colleen

Colleen is obviously flustered that she was late to this important lunch. She apologizes a few too many times as she sips her iced tea and orders a salad. Mike takes the opportunity to put her mind at ease and coach her on her communication skills at the same time. He doesn't mind the effort, and he makes a mental note that this overapologizing is something he will work on with her once she joins the team. It is weak behavior that rarely helps improve a negative situation. He's confident she will accept today's offer, and this will be the first of many coaching scenarios for the two of them.

"Colleen, I accept your apology. You were late. You said you were sorry. It's over." Mike looks at her directly and pauses. His message is clear: *Your continuous apologies are ruining the positive moment here, so please stop it.* After a moment he smiles. "Besides, we've got to get to the details of our meeting today and that offer I'm going to be making to you."

Colleen flushes slightly at Mike's directness, takes a sip of her iced tea, and regains her composure. She folds her arms on the table, leans forward, and says, "You're right. Thank you."

Mike spends the next 10 minutes telling Colleen about his vision of the future for the division over the next five years. He gives her a detailed analysis of how he intends to provide a more compelling set of products and services for current customers, and how those expanded offerings will add new customers every year.

Colleen is impressed with the level of nuance Mike shares about a wide array of both big and small customers. He really knows the value his division provides for each and how they can their expand efforts. He never uses expressions like "customer account penetration" or "market space we occupy." Instead, he just demonstrates how his division helps his customers with their customers and can do even more with greater effort. He shares a wide variety of details that usually only a project manager or an account executive would know. It is energizing. She's so wrapped up in his customers insight, she's no longer embarrassed for being late.

Mike paints a picture of a dynamic, growing division without ever mentioning the numbers that usually litter these conversations. He makes few references to revenue growth, market share, gross margin, or profitability. Instead, Mike's discussion of the future includes a full description of what his division will actually look like with expanded personnel and production capabilities. She can see it unfolding in front of her. She can't wait for the formal offer. She hopes it will be the right number.

He then surprises her. He asks her what she thinks of his growth plans. She is caught off guard, and she's concerned she will say the wrong thing, perhaps ruining her chances.

12:35 James Starts to Negotiate; Chad Is Ready

"Well, thanks for being open to this," James says. "I may be hurting my position with this statement, but I really want to work for you. I'm excited about the possibilities."

"Oh, I promise I won't hold it against you," Chad says. "Please tell me what you have in mind." He is in total control, he thinks; no reason not to sound magnanimous and wise.

"Great, well then let me start off by saying that $73,000 is a fair and reasonable number for many people in the market for a new job. It is a lot of money, these days, especially to work in a great company like yours." James is confident and moves slowly through his reasoning.

"Now, having said that, let me go on and tell you why that number won't work for me. I know this position pays as much as $85,000 in firms for employees with my training and experience. Now, I'm not saying I have to have $85,000 by any means; but I think $82,000 is a salary I could agree to right now."

Chad knows he's right in wanting to bring James on board. This guy is smart, prepared, and eloquent to boot. But he sure as hell isn't going to get $82,000 out of Chad.

"Boy James, that's pretty steep. I'm not saying you're not worth it. Heck, I'd love to pay you that much and get this settled right now," Chad says. "But, unfortunately, budgets are, well, budgets. I can move to $78,000 without going back over my pro formas, which will delay this whole process; and even then it might not work. So, I can meet you at $78,000. Do we have a deal?" Chad is now laying the entire card deck out. This is the number he budgeted for. Now, there's really no wiggle room left.

12:45 Colleen Weighs In

Mike reassures Colleen that she can handle this impromptu assignment. He reminds her of the great insights she made during her first interview, and then again during a tour of their operations center in the second round.

Then, Mike starts asking questions to help her along. He inquires about a number of assignments from her resume that she shared with him during the interview process. He follows up by asking her how she would apply what she learned to the specific customer growth programs he described just a few minutes earlier.

That is all the prodding Colleen needs. As soon as Mike helps her link her past experiences to his plans, she starts to roll. She comes up with several good ideas very quickly, and then asks Mike more about the specifics of his growth plans, industry group by industry group, to help her flush out even more.

Mike knows why they are at this point. Early on, she stumbled by losing composure after she was late. Then, perhaps still self-conscious, she was slow to respond to Mike's open-ended growth scenario. But she recovered and put forth an industry intellect that was worth the price of lunch many times over.

It was the result of Mike's practiced ability to take great mental notes, and then ask questions based on those notes. Colleen shared lots of great professional experiences during her first two interviews. He remembered a number of her specific areas of expertise, and then asked her about them in the context of his growth scenario.

Some people in the company had noticed Mike's unique skills in helping people translate their past experiences and skills into future success. They complimented him about it frequently, telling him he was a great "active listener." He thanked them because he was always gracious in accepting a sincere compliment. But he puzzled about the term "active listener." "If you're not an active listener," he'd joke with his wife, "are you an 'active ignorer'?"

The conversation with Colleen has become even more animated. Suddenly, Mike notices that it is getting late. He has to make the offer and nail things down before he heads off to that tough supplier meeting.

"Colleen, we could go on all afternoon, which would be of tremendous benefit to me," Mike says. "But we need to start paying you for your expertise. We want you to join us so you can become a part of the team and brainstorm like this with us every day."

Colleen feels like she is ready to start the next day, before she even hears the salary. She knows she'll have to give notice to her current boss; but working those last two weeks will be tough with the excitement brewing in Mike's division.

12:46 James Accepts the Offer, but Makes One More Push

James looks down for a full couple of seconds while he considers the $78,000 offer Chad just laid on the table. It's not an uncomfortable silence for either one of them. Chad has given James a lot to think about.

"Chad I want to come to work for you, so I will accept your offer. But I want to ask you for a favor."

Chad is relieved. This is going to work out—and on *his* terms.

"Well, we could argue all day long over the last four thousand dollars. I'll come to work for you for what you offered, because it's a great opportunity and I like your ideas. And it is a very reasonable salary. But I want to come into the fold that very first day, find my way around the office getting used to things, feeling great, and not second-guessing my decision in any way." James takes a long breath and then proceeds. "If you could wring an extra $2,000 out of your budget to get us to $80,000, I'd feel we'd accomplished something very positive. Is that possible?"

Chad isn't prepared for this, so he just delivers a knee-jerk question, "But you're not holding my feet to the fire. You will move over to us for the $78,000? That's right, isn't it?"

"Yes, I will Chad, that's right, I will. And I won't complain about it later, either," James continued. "But I want to feel rock solid about this decision without any self-doubt. Eighty K gets me that piece of mind. It's not much in the long run for either one of us, and I know that. But it will help me to hit the bricks running with you and have the best attitude possible."

Chad likes James's approach and reasoning capabilities on the sticky discussion of pay. Many of Chad's employees show discomfort during salary talks. Not James. He is cool and rational and shows he understands that salaries are not personal, just budget issues. Chad also likes the fact that James formally accepted the offer and then made a compelling argument for the extra bit of money. Chad makes a snap decision to find the money to get James on board.

"James, I enjoy your style and I like your smarts. I'll have to juggle a bit, but we want you and your energy on our side. Eighty grand it is."

The two shake hands and go over the final details of James's starting date. James is very happy with the way he was treated by Chad.

Chad is fired up. True, he had to bend quite a bit, but James is a star. He has a bounce in his step as he heads for his car to meet with that tough supplier.

12:54 Mike Makes the Offer

Mike is now ready to extend a formal offer to Colleen. Last week, after Colleen's second great interview and tour, he asked his HR manager to come up with a salary range for Colleen. He looked at it over the weekend. As with James, someone like Colleen is commanding top dollar of $85,000 at a few companies, but her pay is pegged between $75,000 and $80,000 for most strong candidates. That is plenty of information for Mike. He knows just how he will handle it.

"Colleen, we want you at our company and at my division. I'd like to offer you the job we've been discussing at a salary of $78,000. I've done my homework and I know you could probably do better and you could do worse as you look at other companies. But here's one thing I want you to consider." Mike pauses for a moment, then continues, "As you were on your tour of our place last week, everyone you met received a raise of at least 2 percent last year. Some high achievers even receive a base increase of 5 percent. I'm very proud of this, based on what's happening with the economy. We need stronger and stronger people like you to keep growing both revenue and profit," Mike says.

"That's why I want you to join us as soon as possible. A year from now, I look forward to us meeting here, going over your performance review and your new higher base pay. While I can't promise that will happen, because I can't predict exactly how much success we'll have in the next year, I am very confident in our plan and in your abilities. What do you think?"

Colleen had gone into the meeting determined to convince Mike she was worth $80,000 in salary. She anticipated she'd get a nice offer from Mike at the lunch. Earlier, as she was running late to get to the lunch, she was determined to fight hard for that number.

But, as soon as Mike lobbed the ball back into her court, she knew she'd take the offer as it stood. Why fight for $2,000 when Mike painted such a compelling picture of success? $78,000 was a fair salary anywhere; it was a great salary at a dynamic company, with an inspiring boss.

"Mike, you've got yourself a new employee," Colleen says. They shake hands and agree to go over the final details tomorrow morning at 8 AM. Mike knows he hasn't picked up any time and will still be late for the supplier meeting. But it's well worth it to him.

12:00 PM

Don't Be That Boss Lessons

12:01 Chad Offers an Olive Branch

✓ Powerful communicators "walk the walk." When they admit a mistake, they do not fall back into "did so, did not" communication.

12:06 Mike Finds the Shoe on the Other Foot

✓ It's okay to be angry with others for missed appointments or deadlines, but use the moment to learn and improve your own skill set, instead of lashing out.

(continued)

(*continued*)

12:15 Chad Makes His Case

✓ When you focus on numbers and data instead of the value and purpose, you wind up negotiating poorly.

12:20 Mike Paints His Picture of the Future for Colleen

✓ Stress stories and images of future success or failure rather than relying on quantifying goals only with revenue, gross margin, and profit numbers.

12:35 James Starts to Negotiate; Chad Is Ready

✓ Be direct and open and resist the urge to posture regarding money issues with employees.

12:45 Colleen Weighs In

✓ You strengthen your connections to your employees when you ask them to discuss their pictures of success for your team as well as sharing your own.

12:46 James Accepts the Offer, but Makes One More Push

✓ You run out of negotiating options by focusing solely on salary numbers instead of performance and vivid goals.

12:54 Mike Makes the Offer

✓ Numbers take on more value when they are supported by meaningful and connective communication.

1:00 PM
Vendor Negotiations:
Winning When You Don't Have the Strongest Hand

1:03 Mike Preps Kim and Himself

Mike jumps into his car in the parking lot of the restaurant where he just finished the successful lunch with Colleen. He turns the ignition but leaves his car in park. He pulls out his BlackBerry and uses his thumb to turn the power back on. He had turned it off as he saw Colleen enter the restaurant and put it in his suit coat breast pocket during the lunch.

He lowers the volume on the Phil Woods sax solo he was listening to on his way over to meet Colleen and begins to check his messages. Both Kim and Jonathan—the vendor he is meeting—had called him back. They both received his calls explaining he would be late. The meeting is still on track. He relaxes some and decides to call back Kim to go over the game plan one more time.

"Hi Kim, this is Mike, thanks for letting me know you got the message." Mike holds his BlackBerry up to his ear. It's not very comfortable, even when he isn't driving. For months he'd been admiring Chad's Jawbone earpiece, but he had never gotten around to picking one up or even ordering one online.

"That's fine, Mike. Did you have a successful lunch with Colleen?" Kim, like all of the managers in the department, knows whenever Mike is about to add to the team. He keeps them abreast of not only his hires, but also his off-site meetings throughout the day. He wants his staff to know where he is and what he's doing. That way, they can judge whether or not to disturb him with a phone call.

"Yes, I did. She'll be on board with us the week after next. It was a great lunch," Mike says. "Listen, I want to go over the game plan for our presentation to Jonathan one more time."

"Oh, I'm ready, Mike," Kim says. He preps his managers for all of their presentations thoroughly to raise their chances of success. Kim continues, "I'll keep the numbers to a minimum and the pictures and stories in which we describe how we are growing to a maximum."

Mike has been working with Kim to dump her "just the facts, ma'am" communication approach, which hurt connections with employees and vendors. It has been a struggle. Kim continually defaults to numbers, charts, and graphs. She told Mike it is frustrating to her that if she takes the trouble to lay everything out, those listening should at least be able to "put two and two together."

"You're right about that," Mike would assure her. "But sticking to being right instead of being good is standing in the way of you becoming a stronger leader. You've obviously worked hard at the numbers. Now, work a little more and tell them what the numbers mean. That's the difference between being right and being good."

Kim would scoff, "I hate all this feel-good stuff," but she understood. Mike would lay on a little harder, "Kim, please don't look at it as 'feel-good stuff.' It's not. It's the type of work real leaders accept as the price of building connections and achieving greater performance from those they rely on."

For the first five or six times, Kim would often respond with "whatever," but she would still follow through on Mike's specific instructions. However, in the last month or so, she had accepted the coaching without the sarcasm. Mike is pleased at Kim's progress.

"I'm going to let you lay everything out," Mike says into his BlackBerry, "then I'm going to take the lead and ask Jonathan about what his plans are for his company. Feel free to join in along the way during my part."

"I will," says Kim. "I'm not shy, and I like how Jonathan has positioned his business. See you in a few."

"Great, see you in a few," says Mike. He clicks off the call and turns the audio on Phil Woods's saxophone back up just a little while he goes over in his head what probing questions he will ask Jonathan. Even though Mike is a powerful communicator, he once again takes time to prepare mentally for his upcoming meeting.

1:10 Chad and Randy Unveil Their Request

Chad pulls up into the parking space next to Randy's car and rolls down his passenger window, "Hey, Randy, how long have you been waiting?"

"Just a minute or two," Randy says. "I was going over the final stuff that Phil sent. He did a good job of getting his stats in. The numbers are now complete," Randy reports. Chad is relieved that he made peace with Phil. This meeting now has a better chance of succeeding.

"How do you handicap our chances of success with Tracy?" Randy asks as the two head toward the main entrance of their vendor's building.

"It's going to be tough with her, based on what we're going to present. But, no matter what, we'll emphasize to her that we're a player in the industry. Eventually, she's going to have to cut us a break," Chad explains. "I think we've got a fifty-fifty shot at getting something out of her today." Chad's insight is good, and his response to Randy is clear. Even if they don't get what they want today, he is smart to stay in front of her.

Tracy's company is the leading vendor of the suppliers critical to the success of Chad's division. Everything they do is superior: top-notch production, on-time delivery, and a small but innovative R&D department. Tracy's company keeps Chad's division looking good with its customers every quarter.

But there's a problem. Chad's division is smaller than many of its top competitors, who wind up getting more attention and preferred treatment from Tracy's team. Mike and Randy have set up the meeting with Tracy in hopes of seeing a faster turnaround time on shipments and a slightly lower price.

Last quarter, Chad spent a good deal of time on the phone with Tracy; but he couldn't get her to budge an inch. "Listen, Chad," Tracy explained, "I love you guys. You're good to work with and you process our invoices promptly. And you are one focused son of a gun, Chad. But look at it from my point of view." She made a powerful argument that she had to keep her priorities on her highest volume customers. "If you ordered more," she says, "I could move you up in the production pecking order and even look at our pricing. But you're not there yet."

Both Chad and Randy like the fact Tracy doesn't play games. She's direct and professional. She's also fair. Tracy agreed to look everything over again once Chad had his purchasing budget set for next year.

Now, three months later after Chad's last plea for a better delivery schedule and lower pricing, the two of them are sitting in Tracy's office, ready to go over the numbers and plead their case. Chad has a lot more confidence in their presentation with Phil's West Coast numbers in his reports.

"Guys, I hear you're weathering the storm out there pretty well. Congrats." Tracy isn't one for small talk, but she is always polite. Chad notices she started out with a sincere compliment that demonstrates she is following the market. She puts them at ease, even though she's in the driver's seat at this meeting.

"Yes, we are, Tracy." Chad jumps in. "We're not growing as quickly as a type A personality like me would like, but we are holding our own."

"All you Ivy League guys are type A, aren't you Chad?" Tracy turns to Randy, "But mere foot soldiers like us," Tracy nods at Randy, "who don't carry the weight of the world on our shoulders, will live longer, won't we Randy?" She smiles at both of them.

Yikes! This is a pretty good jab at Chad. While Randy mutters, "Sure, I guess so," Chad resists the urge to correct her—his alma maters, Williams and Northwestern's Kellogg School of Business, are not Ivy League institutions—and instead smiles weakly, wondering why Tracy is giving it to him. What did he do to offend her so quickly?

Randy doesn't nod or wink to Tracy. That would be breaking ranks. But he knows why she's poking at Chad, who never seems to catch on that his not-so-subtle self-promotion is irritating. Chad is always giving himself labels that sound like he just came from a self-affirmation seminar. Today Chad called himself "type A personality"; but it just as easily could have been "leader of the 'go-to' team," or the guy who believes that "failure is not an option."

Randy feels that Tracy is indeed a pretty smart cookie. She knows that Chad and he are sitting there, mutual hats in hand. She doesn't want to start the meeting letting Chad get away with his promotional crap. Randy also finds himself wondering what it would be to like to work for someone as insightful as Tracy.

1:21 Mike Lets Kim Take the Lead

"Thanks for your flexibility, Jonathan. I got behind and I couldn't catch up," Mike says to Jonathan as he and Kim got settled in their supplier's small office.

"That's okay, Mike, I understand. It gave me a chance to do a few extra things," Jonathan says.

Kim marvels once again at Mike's leadership and skill. It would have been easy for him to throw that new hire under the bus. After all, it's Colleen's fault that Mike was running late. Instead, he just simply apologized and didn't trouble Jonathan with the reasons. *Elegant,* Kim thinks. *It's an elegant way to get back on track quickly.*

"Jonathan, your products are critical to our success with our clients. We want more of them, faster, and we want to pay less for it. We're here to ask you for a couple of things," Mike says. "First, we want a shipment schedule of 14 days instead of the 21-day schedule we've been on with you for a year or so. Second, we are looking for a price cut of 5 percent. We've done our homework and we hope to get you over to our way of thinking. Both requests will be good for your company, as well as ours."

Jonathan smiles. "Boy, Mike, you don't mess around, do you? Okay, I knew you were going to ask for something; but I didn't know it would be so specific. Well, I'm not agreeing to anything yet, and I won't promise that I will, either. But I'm willing to listen. And thanks for admitting you need us. Most of our customers would never say something like that when they're asking for a price break," Jonathan says.

Kim is again amazed at how quickly Mike gets Jonathan's attention and starts a negotiation with such positive vibes—even after he was late for the meeting. She makes a strong mental note: Mike is a great boss because he rarely, if ever, blames others for his problems, even when others affect his performance.

"Then I'm happy we're off to a good start," Mike says. "And now it's going to get even better. I'm going to have Kim take over and present our plan for the next couple of years."

"Thanks, Mike," Kim says. "Jonathan, we plan everything we do around what our customers need to make their customers happy. We say that our mission, vision, and values are determined by whether we're succeeding in helping our customers to be in great shape with *their* customers. As long as we do that, we figure we're going to stay in the picture and grow for a long time."

Kim goes on to explain to Jonathan how all their growth opportunities focus on a detailed examination of *their customers' growth opportunities*. She uses five different examples in five different market sectors to demonstrate how this plan led to steady increases in sales and gross margin in the last two years. Then she talks about what they were doing this quarter—and had planned for the next quarter—to come up with several new market segments to go after once they understood their future customers' customers.

While Kim did include several critical sales figures and buying projections along the way, they were all there to punctuate the happy ending to another customer story. She would have been much more comfortable beefing up this report with at least three times as much data justifying her conclusions, but she knew Mike would have told her to take it all out. She had the data memorized, though, just in case Jonathan questioned anything.

It's an unusual presentation for Jonathan to sit through. Usually, customers and suppliers came in for meetings with lots of spreadsheets and charts regarding market expansion or contraction, costs per unit of production, and quality control figures. Kim only talks about her customers, using a simple PowerPoint presentation that featured a single clear text headline or main idea on each projected slide and minimal graphics. It's easy to follow, especially as Kim becomes more and more excited about the success her customers are having.

Mike sits quietly but attentively. He never takes his eyes off Kim and her presentation slides. He knows that if he concentrates on what Kim was saying, it will set the tone and also a visual tableau for Jonathan to stay tuned in as well. Mike coaches all of his managers to focus attention on the speaker in all customer meetings, despite the intense urge to peruse their notes or even glance at an incoming e-mail on a BlackBerry.

He's taking mental notes along the way. He realizes that Kim has come a long way in the last year. She's really connecting with Jonathan. As a result, Jonathan is gaining a clear and compelling insight into what Mike's division is up to and why it's different from the much larger players against whom they compete.

Mike worked hard with Kim to get her to this point. As an engineer, she had been trained that the more detailed facts, figures, and data she could present in a meeting, the better for everyone involved. Using a consistent and strong hand during brief coaching sessions following each of her production meetings, Mike had pushed Kim to concentrate more on what the numbers mean for everyone in the room. He told her it was a low percentage tactic (he figured she would love his choice of words) to merely spout number after number and hope everyone could connect the dots as easily as she did. It was the same type of firm and unending coaching he delivered to all of his key managers.

Mike didn't let up on Kim, despite all of her hard work and obvious talent. It led to more than one tiff between them along the way. "So you're telling me I've got to dumb it down for everyone, aren't you? Even experienced engineers pulling in over 85,000 bucks a year?" She was almost spitting with frustration.

"No, I want you to show them the power of your numbers so they'll follow your lead and direction," Mike said quietly after a pause. "Otherwise, you might as well just send them an e-mail and attach a spreadsheet. When you talk to your team, you've got to connect to them if you expect them to do what you need them to. Make the numbers *mean* something. Give them a specific value that demonstrates how they're helping our customers, every time you present to your team. Do that and you're starting to act like a boss who people will want to work for, instead of one who's merely smart."

Then Mike delivered a devastating blow to Kim. He had prepared for this moment, waiting as she kept pushing back after every coaching session. "Kim, you are a bright engineer, but I can find bright engineers anywhere. You are a hardworking manager. But you'll never be as successful as you want to be unless you take the time and exert the mental calories to make your words meaningful, to everyone."

Kim started to say something—once and then twice—but she never finished the sentence. Instead, she took a long pause, and said, "You're right Mike, I'm going to get better at this. I want to be a stronger leader."

That breakthrough was about eight months ago. Since then, she'd improved in every meeting and had made even more strides as head of the strategic planning process.

Today Mike had granted her another great opportunity. The meeting with Jonathan wasn't critical, but it gave her a chance to demonstrate her leadership skills to others, outside of the company. She's succeeding. Jonathan is sitting forward and engaged from the first slide. He stops her frequently to ask questions.

Mike pauses to savor the moment. Kim has not only gone from being a strong employee who completed tasks successfully to a strong leader who can coach others to complete successful tasks, now she's also showing a key supplier that Mike's division is deep in talent.

1:23 Chad Hands the Reins to Randy, but Doesn't Let Go

Chad flushes at Tracy's pointed sarcasm, but he ignores it. He is a "go-to" guy, he'll tell himself at a time like this. He'll just power through, not sweating what he considers the small stuff.

"Tracy, I'm going to let Randy handle the bulk of our discussion today. I'm just here to show you how important our relationship with you is and how much we're counting on your help," Chad says.

Tracy nods and smiles. She doesn't believe for a second that Chad will really keep his mouth shut for long. Randy is thinking the same thing.

"Tracy, as you mentioned, we're having a pretty decent year, despite everything going on," Randy starts. "And next year we're looking at more improvement in all areas, which is why we're here to chat with you."

Randy starts running through detailed sales and financial statistics that he and Chad carefully prepared. It's a ton of financial and market information, with chart after chart filling the screen. The first couple of times that Randy made a minor mistake in his delivery—or pointed to the wrong cell on the screen—Chad kept silent. He even patted himself on the back for allowing Randy to be a star.

Then Randy comes to the critical part of the presentation. "Tracy, we've completed our projections for the next four quarters and we want you to know we'll be ordering more from you next year—as much as 8 percent more, in fact, according to purchasing forecasts I've collated for our different regions."

Chad can't hold himself back. "Hey, Randy, may I jump in for just a minute to clarify just a point or two?" Chad is pleased at his polite request.

I knew he couldn't keep quiet, thinks Tracy. *Randy is handling himself well. He's sharp and well spoken, even when he's laying the data on too thick. I wonder if he's happy working for Chad?*

"Of course, Chad. Please go ahead," Randy says, surprised Chad has let him go this far without butting in.

"To tell you the truth, Tracy," Chad begins, "Randy is underselling this a little bit. Probably just due to his modest nature, I guess."

Chad is a real piece of work, Tracy thinks. *First he interrupts his guy after he claims that he won't. Next he slaps his guy right in front of me and tries to make it better with a lame, back-handed compliment. Well, let's see how badly Randy screwed up to deserve this. Not much, I bet,* she thinks.

"That magenta line labeled with 8 percent, which demonstrates our projected purchases from you for next year, actually represents a real increase of 8.42 percent. Randy must have rounded down in displaying his calculations," Chad explains, and turns to Randy. "Hey, Randy, that's okay, I do it all the time. You've really done a great job explaining to Tracy where we stand. I'm impressed," Chad says.

Wow, an order of oversized ego with a side of condescension to boot, thinks Tracy. She is unimpressed with the difference 8 percent and 8.42 percent makes to their argument.

"No, you're right, Chad. Please, proceed with this." Randy says, correctly predicting his time in the spotlight for this meeting has come to ignominious end.

"Okay, thanks, I'll just wrap up, if that's okay," Chad says—relieved to be back in the driver's seat.

1:50 Mike Starts Asking Jonathan Questions

Kim completes her customer-focused stories with a simple slide with a number on the screen:

Our Projected Dollar Order Increases: 8.42 Percent

"So, Jonathan, this is our case for the price break and faster delivery schedule. We're going to be helping our customers serve their customers better and better in the months and years ahead," says Kim. "That's why we want you to agree to a shipment schedule of 14 days instead of the 21-day schedule we've been on with you for a year or so. That, along with a price cut of 5 percent, would help us to help our customers and become a stronger industry player in the process."

Good finish, Kim! Mike wants to scream with joy. She followed all of Mike's rules for a powerful end to any presentation. She repeated "the ask"—what she wanted from Jonathan—with a very similar cadence and words to the ones Mike had used as the meeting started.

Mike is especially proud that Kim did not make reference to the fact that she was repeating something Mike had already said. This is a huge communication breakthrough for Kim. She, worse than most of the people who work for him, had used the expressions "Let me repeat" and "As I said before" ad nauseum in all of her meetings. Mike had ordered, pushed, and even begged her to stop using these expressions.

"Repetition is great. Repeat. Repeat. Repeat to get your headline or directive across," Mike preached." But do not *draw attention* to the fact you are repeating. That ruins everything. You sound like you're a stern school marm or a nagging parent when you do."

Kim must have finally gotten the message, because she ends this presentation to Jonathan with a bang. Now it's Mike's turn. But he doesn't jump in immediately. He waits for Jonathan to comment.

"Nice job, Kim," Jonathan says, "very impressive mission and execution. You guys are definitely on your way to making your mark with that 'helping your customer with their customers' thing. I like it." Then he pauses and turns to Mike. "Well, I'm ready to respond to your request, unless you have something to add."

"Well, I don't have something to add," Mike says quietly, "but I do have some questions for you." He then spends the next 10 minutes asking insightful and pointed questions about the mission and future plans for Jonathan's business. He follows up Jonathan's initial responses with additional questions that demonstrate his understanding and concern for Jonathan's market position. The questions are so well researched that Jonathan is flattered about the homework his customer has done on his operation. That, coupled with Kim's compelling presentation, sets the stage for Jonathan's response to their request.

"Okay, guys. I'm a fan. I was before you walked in, and even more so now," Jonathan begins. "As for the shipping terms, you've got it. As of tomorrow's orders, you'll have the 14 days, just like our top customers. It's easy to see we have to move product to you so you can keep your customers and their customers happy. I'm not going to move on price right now, though, because these are just your projections. Even if you hit these numbers, you still won't crack our top 20 customer list.

"But I'm going to give you a goal to shoot for," Jonathan continues. "If you guys hit this over 8 percent increase for three straight months, I'm going to give you your price break for the next three months. As long as you keep the increases steady and on track with what you've promised, you'll enjoy the discount. If your orders slip—even for a month—we'll have to start over again. How does that suit you?"

It's a solid win, Mike thinks. "It suits us just fine, Jonathan. Thanks for your time and your help."

"You're welcome, Mike," Jonathan says. "Kim, I found your presentation creative and easy to follow. Believe me, I sit through them all day, and yours was a delight."

"Thank you, Jonathan," Kim says. "Can we come back in six months and do it all again? We might have some more surprises for you."

"You bet. You have my number," Jonathan says.

Mike is beaming as he walks to the car. Six months ago, Kim had deflected every compliment with averted eyes and the lame-sounding, "Just doin' my job." Not only had she performed incredibly well this time, but she also accepted a compliment gracefully and used that positive karma from Jonathan to ask for a follow-up meeting. Kim is becoming a strong leader very quickly.

1:52 Tracy Bursts the Bubble

"Okay, guys, you came here for an answer. And I've got one for you. It's the old good-news, bad-news deal," Tracy says. "Bad news first: I can't move on price or shipping dates. Your projected increase is great. We appreciate the business, and we're glad you're moving forward with more for us. But you're still not in our top 20 customers. I can't even consider helping you until I see these numbers pan out for at least two quarters. I hope you understand."

"Sure, Tracy, we do," Chad says. "But you said there was some good news?"

"Yeah, there is," Tracy says. "You guys know your stuff. Randy, your numbers were organized and thorough. I want to give you another shot in six months. Come back then and we'll look at your actual orders and further projections and we'll see about that discount. I can tell you it won't be as low as you're asking, but we may be able to move in your direction."

"Fair enough, Tracy," agrees Chad. They all shake hands.

"As usual, it's been an honor and a privilege, Tracy," Chad says on the way out.

"Sure has, Chad," Tracy turns to her computer as they leave her office. *Chad, you should really dial it down a notch or two,* she thinks when they were gone.

1:00 PM

Don't Be That Boss Lessons

1:03 Mike Preps Kim and Himself

✓ Spend time with your B+ and A– players, pushing them to improve their communication skills even though they may already be a strong asset to the management team.

1:10 Chad and Randy Unveil Their Request

✓ Don't use adjectives to describe yourself. Good bosses let others come to their own conclusions.

1:21 Mike Lets Kim Take the Lead

✓ Coach your employees vigorously to improve their communication skills; and then allow them to demonstrate what they have learned.

(continued)

(*continued*)

1:23 Chad Hands the Reins to Randy, but Doesn't Let Go

✓ Resist the urge to correct your employees in front of others outside of your company. It makes you and the employee appear to be weak.

1:50 Mike Starts Asking Jonathan Questions

✓ Asking meaningful questions builds rapport and increases connections, especially when you follow up with even better questions.

1:52 Tracy Busts the Bubble

✓ Unless you're having a sit-down with the President of the United States, the Pope, or the Dalai Lama, don't end a meeting with the words, "it has been an honor," because it's just not true.

2:00 PM
Disciplining an Employee:
Hit Them with Specifics or Don't Hit Them at All

2:03 Chad Reaches Out to Mike

Best-selling authors Larry Bossidy and Ram Charan are still chatting about *Execution* on Chad's CD player as he pulls out of the parking lot of Tracy's building to head back to his office. Choosing to stop his continuing business education for a minute, he turns down the volume on the *Execution* guys and takes stock of the day. It isn't an uplifting experience.

First, there was the mess at the dry cleaners; then there was the dust-up with Phil, which had ended okay, but was a definite loss because Lynne was now monitoring the situation. The sales and financial meetings had plodded along but were nothing special. The strategic planning update was a minor loss. His team was behind on the goals they had all agreed upon. The Steve Moreno meeting was a disaster. It's never good when the customer bites your head off in front of one of your employees. He had to admit lunch was no better than a draw. He landed James, but wound up paying more than he had anticipated. Chad wondered what, if anything, he could have done to get James on board, feeling great, at the right budget number.

Then there was Tracy. This meeting was the most confusing to Chad. The result was fine; they were hoping for her to move on price and delivery, but didn't count on it. She listened, agreed they were doing well, and agreed to keep listening. Overall, that was a minor accomplishment. But, as he replays Tracy's small biting comments, he becomes concerned—that she seemed far more connected to Randy than to him. In terms of business hierarchy, Chad and Tracy should have been in perfect sync; they were both the bosses. *This is not a successful day,* Chad realizes. And he had vowed he would make it great after that lousy 360 on Friday. That's not how it's working out. He puts his Jawbone in his ear, picks up his BlackBerry, and hits Mike's number on speed dial.

"Hey, man, how's your Monday?" Chad starts.

"Well, I'm happy to report the week is off to a good start," Mike responds, "but I've got a dismal chore coming up. I've got to have one of those final warning talks with one of my guys. I don't enjoy them, but it's an important part of being the boss."

This is why Chad enjoys their friendship. Mike is never full of it. Chad knows if Mike says he had a good morning, there is a definite reason for it. Then Mike shares his trepidation about his next meeting. Mike gave a good, brief update and shared something about his current state of mind as well.

"I've got one of those coming up next as well," Chad shares. "Why don't these people just do what they are supposed to do, like we do?"

"Well, if they did, maybe we wouldn't have jobs, would we? Or even worse, maybe they'd be our bosses," Mike says.

"Yeah, you're right," Chad says, realizing Mike had commiserated with him but did not share the same complaints about his employees. Chad worries that Mike thinks he's whining—which, he admits to himself, he is.

"Listen, I'm calling to ask you for a favor," Chad continues. "I'm determined to get a better 360 next time, and I wanted to know if you could give me some big-time help."

"Sure," says Mike. "What do you need?"

"I know it's short notice, but do you have time to come to my production meeting at four today?" Chad asked. "I want you to watch what I'm doing and give me some pointers on the communications front. You're so much better at this stuff than I am; and I've got to pick up my game or I'm going to be working for you way sooner than I'll want to be."

This is a very flattering and sincere request. Chad is a sharp guy and a good friend. Mike tells him he can make it work.

2:15 Mike Spells It Out for Gary

When he gets back to the office, Mike checks his messages and drops a quick e-mail to Jeanie on the West Coast telling her that the numbers she sent had been very helpful. Mike is good at circling back with his employees. Jeanie deserves to be kept in the loop.

Then he takes a breath and leaves his office to find Gary. Out of all of his "boss chores," this is the one Mike finds most daunting. He has to have the final chat with an employee whose performance has dipped so low that he and everybody in the division knows he has one foot out the door.

Over the last few months, Mike has had to fight the urge to devote too much energy to Gary. His natural inclination was to pour a ton of work into saving an underachiever like Gary, who everyone recognizes as a bright and likable fellow. As Mike matured as a leader, he'd come to realize that wasting an inordinate amount of effort on your C– players meant you weren't spending nearly enough time with the Bs and As who were producing for you. That always led to poorer team performance and resentment from the successful employees.

Mike had invested just the appropriate amount of coaching time with Gary—depressingly, without significant improvement. He had followed all the proper human resources protocols leading up to the meeting.

He approaches Gary's cubicle. "Gary, I need to speak to you. I'd like you to please come with me to my office now." Mike has practiced everything he was going to say to Gary, including this opening salvo. He didn't ask Gary the facetious "Do you have a minute?" as he had done with many other employees with whom he'd had "the final talk." It was a ridiculous question, Mike finally realized. The employee almost always knew what was coming. What choice did they have? "No, I don't have time for a final trip to the woodshed, boss"?

Mike decides to unwrap his final warning speech to Gary without any of the tired bromides bosses had been using for years. After this meeting Mike wants Gary to leave his office, not a "dead man walking," but rather someone who knows exactly what steps he will have to take in what time frame in order to keep his job.

Mike has the typical "boss office" furniture. There's a decent-sized desk with two side chairs in front of it and his bigger, more comfortable chair behind it. In the corner, there's a small worktable with two more chairs. He only sits behind his desk when he's working on the computer or talking on his phone. He has every discussion with employees and corporate colleagues either at his worktable or in the two side chairs in front of his desk.

Mike offers the "you first" gesture and steps aside to let Gary into his office. Then he motions for Gary to sit in one of the side chairs in front of his desk and deliberately shuts the door slowly so they can have privacy and to underscore the gravity of the discussion.

"This is going to be a difficult meeting," Mike starts in as soon as he sits down. "I'm going to tell you four things about your performance that must improve right away, or I'm going to have to let you go. And Gary, when I say right away—I mean today. Your job is at risk right now and every day until you get to where you need to be in terms of performance. Let's get started."

Mike does not allude to the fact they had been over these and other performance issues items before. Unlike most other bosses, Mike feels that reminding failing employees standing at the point of no return that they had been warned repeatedly is a waste of time. Besides, it has all been documented in the HR paper trail. This meeting isn't about Mike covering his rear end on the labor rules front. Instead, it's a reasonable last attempt to help save Gary's job. Besides, Gary shouldn't have to be reminded this was well-trod ground. If he didn't know why he was sitting across from Mike, he'd have to be in serious denial.

Mike knows exactly what his job is for the next 20 minutes or so. He is there to give targeted coaching that will lead to immediate, measurable performance to save Gary from being fired. He also hopes to save his own division the considerable expense of severance and then hiring someone else for Gary's slot. Though Mike's forte isn't numbers, he knows that high turnover not only hurts morale and productivity, it's just flat-out expensive on the monthly P&L.

Gary sits up straight and pays close attention while Mike spells out in detailed terms four recent instances in which Gary either missed a deadline or turned in substandard work. Mike has his facts straight and goes slowly through each episode since their last discussion about Gary's poor performance last month. And, unlike most bosses in a meeting like this, Mike has prepared what he was going to say—and is very specific in the examples he gives.

- Instead of saying, "You act like you don't care about your job here," he says, "You were late to meetings three times in the last three weeks, including this morning. We all had to wait for you to get going. That's a huge waste of resources and creates a ton of tension in the room as well."

- Instead of saying, "You cop an attitude with Kim when she assigns tasks," he says, "Last week, you battled Kim over her assignments in the conference room without making specific objections that could be professionally debated. You just said the plan was 'poorly conceived,' almost under your breath, without backing it up or offering an alternative. That's just whining and poor performance from you."

Mike walks a fine line in this, the most difficult part of "the talk." He is disappointed and angry with Gary. Gary could perform better, and they both know it. But Mike had decided early on that his goal was not to explain his personal feelings about the sorry state of affairs that led to this meeting, but rather to help Gary succeed. Mike knows his emotions, good or bad, aren't relevant. This is all about improving Gary's performance for the division.

2:18 Chad Follows Up with Lynne

Just like Mike, Chad has a final tough talk meeting coming up next in his schedule. But he wants to let his boss Lynne know he was good with Phil, before the day goes on much longer. He picks up his phone and dials Susan's extension.

"Hey, Susan," Chad says. "Could you stop by my office in about 10 minutes? I have a few things I'd like to go over with you."

"Oh, ah, sure," Susan says. Her voice begins to crack, "Umm, really, I can come down the hall right now. There's nothing pressing on my desk, really."

"No, 10 minutes will work just fine," Chad says. He is so focused on the e-mail he has to compose to Lynne, he doesn't realize Susan is scared to death that she is about to be fired.

"Um, okay," says Susan. "Should I bring any reports or anything?" She, like everyone in the division, knows Chad loves to go over numbers and is forever asking for more data. She is hoping he wants some information and doesn't want to talk about her performance.

"No, I don't think so. Just show up in about 10," Chad says, letting Susan know this conversation is over.

"Okay, sure," says Susan. She hangs up the phone and notices that her hand is shaking. She hurries to the restroom to collect herself. Chad has no idea she's petrified.

Then Chad turns to his computer and quickly pounds out an e-mail to Lynne.

Re: Re: NEED PROJECTIONS YOU PROMISED!!!

Lynne:

Good news. Phil and I hashed it all out. We're good.

Not only that, he worked some magic with his schedule and got the numbers to me that I needed in time for the meeting with my vendor, which went very well. I want to apologize for the fact this had to muddy up your day. It was my fault. I didn't handle things very well with Phil. I'm still learning.

Thanks,

Chad

This is new territory for Chad. Technically, this mess wasn't his fault. It was Phil's for not hitting the deadline he had promised. But Chad realizes he'd taken Phil's relatively minor miscue and created a forest fire with his over-the-top e-mail. *I've really got to be nicer,* thinks Chad, as he pulls up his notes on Susan. He misses the point completely, though; niceness has nothing to do with it. Susan pokes her head in the doorway.

"Now?" she asks.

"Yes, now, please come in and sit down," Chad says, all smiles.

2:27 Gary Gets No Sympathy from Mike

"Mike, you're right. In fact, you're 100 percent right," Gary responds. "I've been seriously underperforming on all fronts. You guys shouldn't ever have to wait on me. That's just silly on my part. And yeah, I had some ideas for Kim, to steer things in another direction, you know, but I just didn't have the energy to spit them out. You know, with all that I'm going through."

Gary is going through a divorce. He and his wife of 12 years are headed to court over a wide variety of issues, including custody of their two children. Because of this, Gary has been spending way too much time on the phone with his lawyer. In addition, he has a new romantic relationship that is creating even more havoc in his personal life. Gary isn't the strong and silent type. He freely shares all of his travails with anyone in the office who will listen.

Mike pauses and slowly delivers his response. "Gary, what you are going through doesn't matter to me when I measure your performance. It can't help me and others here succeed. I'm not happy things are a mess for you right now at home, but I can't take that into consideration. It won't help me, and it won't help you."

"Ouch," Gary quickly responds. "I never took you for the 'ice water in the veins' type of guy. Can't you see I'm struggling here?"

"Sure I can," Mike smiles, "and because my blood always flows through my veins at just the right temperature, I want to share something with you. We have a great team here, and you're still a part of it. When you walk into the office, I want you to realize this is one place where you can succeed every single day, no matter what is going on out there in your life. Even when everything else is lousy, *you* can still be great when you're here."

"Okay, you're right . . . absolutely," Gary says. "But it's just I have such a hard time concentrating on all of our projects when I keep thinking I may actually lose my kids."

"You're right," says Mike. "And at the same time, if you're going to earn your pay, that means your colleagues, your boss, me, and the owners of the company deserve the full Gary. We're not getting anywhere near that right now. You're getting paid every two weeks like clockwork, and you're getting full benefits as well. In return, you're not delivering anywhere near what we're investing in you. You're a loss for us right now, and no business can keep losing and survive."

"Yeah, but . . ." Gary begins.

Mike holds up his hands, asking Gary to stop. "Gary, the next time you miss a deadline or show up late for a meeting, here's what's going to happen. I'm going to spend some time in my office squaring things with HR; then I'm going to call you in where we'll have, oh, about a two-minute meeting. It's going to be short because I'm going to fire you; and there won't be a lot for either one of us to say. Someone from HR will be there to document the whole thing, but they won't say much, either. But that's just the start of this lousy episode for both of us."

Mike pauses for a moment to let the scene sink in for Gary.

"Then I'm going to grab a box from shipping and stand right next to you at your desk while you clean it out. My guess is we'll both suffer from the unbelievably awkward silence as you place all your personal stuff including the pictures of your kids in the cardboard box. Then, we'll walk out of the office together. Everyone watching the employment death march will be pretty upset because they really like you here. And that includes me.

But that doesn't matter. If you underperform, you can't work here.

"Finally, I'll walk you out to your car and offer to shake your hand and wish you luck. You'll be so upset, you may elect not to shake my hand, which I would understand. Then you will drive out of the parking lot, and, on top of everything else going on in your life, you'll have to find a job with benefits. It will be a miserable day for you and me."

Mike stops talking. It's time for Gary to respond. "Geez, Mike, you didn't spare a single bloody detail. You've really thought about this, haven't you?"

"You bet," Mike says. "I try to picture exactly how a painful episode will play out when I have to make a difficult decision. And it doesn't get any more difficult than firing someone."

"Okay, is there any hope for this patient, or should I start looking now?" Gary asks. It's a sincere question, without a hint of the passive-aggressive voice Gary had been using earlier in the meeting.

"I want you to work here. And I want you to succeed, starting right now. If I thought the situation was hopeless, we'd be doing the box thing at your desk right now," Mike says.

"Okay, please tell me how I can turn this thing around?" Gary asks.

"You bet. I've given that a lot of thought."

2:29 Chad Treads Very Lightly with Susan

"Please sit down, Susan; right there is fine." Chad motions to his side chair across the desk from his chair, where he remains seated. Chad's office has a more formal feeling than Mike's. He has several pieces of framed artwork, all featuring waterfowl. Mike teases him often, telling him how much he admires Chad for recycling the calendars he got from his insurance agent. It was a good line.

"Susan, I want to start this conversation by saying that you've got to know how much respect I have for you as a person," Chad says. "You have a tremendous amount of talent, which, I can tell you right now, every single one of us admires. We really do."

Susan's worst fears are being realized. He is letting her go and just softening the blow so he won't feel so bad about it. Typical Chad! "Oh, God! Are you firing me, Chad?" Susan asks.

"No, no, I'm not, but we do have some important issues to discuss . . . issues about your performance, okay?" Chad seems to be asking for permission to proceed.

"Sure, Chad," Susan says. "I mean, of course, yes, I want to hear what you have to say."

"Great," says Chad. "Well, let me get back to where I started, and that is that I have tremendous respect for you as a person."

Susan, realizing she is safe for now, finds this choice of words silly, not comforting. "Respect for you as a *person*"—*as opposed to what, Chad,* she thinks, *tremendous respect for me as an amphibian, a reptile, or what?*

Chad continues, "You're very professional in your demeanor in all aspects of your job, and, in many ways, you're a great role model for others in the division. You're always on time and you never complain. That's really been a blessing for me."

"Well, that certainly is nice to hear, Chad." Susan says, very relieved. "Thank you for the compliment." But she is also confused. What is this meeting for? Is she in trouble or not?

"Well, that's exactly why I wanted to chat with you," Chad continues. "It's because you're so professional that I'm troubled by the last three estimates you put together for the production team. They were way off. So much so that we wound up just breaking even on two of them, and actually lost money on the third. That's no way to be profitable, especially in this economic environment. Do you see what I'm getting at?"

"Sure—you want better estimates from me, is that right?" Susan asks, meekly.

"Exactly, that's what I want," Chad says with a bit of triumph in his voice. "And I want you to know that I'm here to help you. I'm pretty good with a spreadsheet every now and then. If you have questions, I'll help you."

"So my job's not on the line, then?" Susan asks.

"Well, I hate to threaten anyone, Susan. That's just not my style." Chad's tone grows very conciliatory. "And I would hate to lose you. But if we can't get these estimates on the money, we're going to have an even tougher conversation next time, okay?" Again he asks for her permission.

Now Susan is really perplexed. What did he mean by "tougher conversation"? Would he fire her, or just put her on some type of double-secret probation? And should she come to him and get his help on the next project estimate, and then the one after that? She isn't sure at all what he's trying to tell her. But she isn't going to ask any additional questions. She isn't fired, and for now, that's good enough.

"Yes, Chad, I understand completely." She doesn't at all.

"Great, well, before we wrap up, there's something else I want to tell you."

Oh, no, thinks Susan. *What now?*

2:36 Mike Shows Gary What Success Looks Like

"Here's what we're going to do, Gary," Mike says. "I'm going to lay out five specific tasks and assignments that you have to score a success with—starting right now. I'm going to monitor your progress week by week. If you hit the mark with every one of them, I'll be able to say your performance is back to where we need you to be."

Mike goes through each of the five in great detail. He paints pictures of success for each of the assignments. He doesn't just give Gary the vague directive "to improve"; instead, Mike gives him highly specific coaching and then describes what a successful outcome looks like or sounds like in each situation.

"I *do* want you to challenge Kim," Mike says. "I'm not asking you to pipe down and dutifully just follow orders. Say what you like and don't like every time. But do it during the meetings, instead of later on when it doesn't help. Be specific about your criticisms and then give a strong alternative that you have thought through. Kim cannot only take it, she'll welcome it, and she'll have you glad to be back in the productive fold again."

When he's through, Mike pauses and slowly asks Gary, "Are you clear on what you have to do to keep your job in each of these tasks? If you aren't, please tell me what you don't understand, and I will work harder to describe success to you."

"No, Mike," replies Gary. "I get it. This is fair. One final question: Do you think I can do this?"

"I know you are capable of following through, but I don't know if you will. It's all up to you whether or not you succeed. I will be rooting for you, though." Mike puts out his hand.

Gary shakes it, nods, and walks out of the office. Gary is shaken, but he is not in doubt about what he has to do to keep his job. There is a voice mail for him from his divorce lawyer when he gets back to his desk. He decides to return the call on his way home from the office. So instead of getting wrapped up with his lawyer for 15 minutes or more, Gary opens up his project file on his desktop.

2:43 Chad Completes the "Criticism Sandwich"

"The final thing I want to tell you is that there is absolutely no doubt in my mind you can do this." Chad says. "You are smart, hardworking, and, like I said, extremely professional. You'll get these estimates right, I'm sure of it. All you need is a little push in the right direction to concentrate more."

Susan smiles. "I'm glad you have faith in me," she says. But she has no idea what he wants her to do differently. She knows about her screwups on the three estimates. But she didn't know precisely what to do differently, besides jumping into Chad's office soon and then often after that to ask for help.

She knows she is professional and hard working; Chad didn't need to tell her that. What she needs to know is how to *specifically* improve her weak performance. She wishes he'd tell her exactly what to do differently, or precisely what she isn't seeing to make the software work for her the way it's supposed to.

Susan is about to pursue these questions when Chad breaks the moment of silence by bringing his hands together in a pseudo clap and belting out, "Well, we seem to be on the same page, Susan. I'm so glad we had a minute to go over this."

"Yes, me too, Chad." They shake hands, and Susan walks out of the office.

Chad sits as his desk and pats himself on the back. He successfully implemented the "criticism sandwich": Give them something positive so they won't take the bad news poorly; tell them what they need to improve; then give them a big boost of confidence going out the door. *Yes,* Chad thinks, *that's really a good way to help an employee, and I performed well in doing it.*

When Susan gets back to her cubicle, she makes sure no one can see her monitor and types in "Monster.com" on Google.

2:00 PM

Don't Be That Boss Lessons

2:03 Chad Reaches Out to Mike

✓ Ask for help from colleagues you trust. It is not a sign of weakness. They will come to your aid, as you will come to theirs.

2:15 Mike Spells It Out for Gary

✓ Lead with a headline in all meetings, especially when the meeting is about poor performance.

2:18 Chad Follows Up With Lynne

✓ Always tie up loose ends involving contentious issues with subordinates and superiors as quickly as possible.

(continued)

(*continued*)

2:27 Gary Gets No Sympathy From Chad

✓ Do not allow employees to manipulate you into accepting poor performance because of their personal issues.

2:29 Chad Treads Very Lightly With Susan

✓ Waiting to deliver a tough message confuses the employee and decreases the opportunity for their turnaround to success.

2:36 Mike Shows Gary What Success Looks Like

✓ Slumping employees have the best chance for success when the boss explains in vivid detail what success looks like in a specific time frame.

2:43 Chad Completes the "Criticism Sandwich"

✓ Kind words do not help the employee or the boss in a conversation about poor performance.

3:00 PM Employee Promotion:

Supervisor Becomes Assistant Manager

3:01 Chad Perceives a Silver Lining

Chad is feeling upbeat after the meeting with Susan. Maybe the day is finally starting to turn around, especially since the next item on his calendar is a breeze. He is going to meet with one of his supervisors and give him a promotion to assistant manager. Chad has had his eye on DeShawn for months now. The time is right to move this guy up and give him more responsibility. Chad is looking forward to the 3:15 meeting, which will be quick and fun. He loves delivering good news.

He now has some time to check his e-mail and his messages. Phil sent a two sentence e-mail asking Chad how the meeting with Susan turned out. Chad sent a quick response, thanking Phil once again. He and Phil are now officially on good terms again.

Then he picks up his office phone to retrieve his voice mail. Ironically, the first voice he hears is from his vendor, Tracy, who must have called right after he got back from the meeting in her office. She didn't say much—just that she wanted to ask him a quick question. But she sure sounded friendly. *Maybe she's reconsidered and will give us that break after all,* thinks Chad. *Maybe the day is going to get even better.*

It won't.

3:02 Mike Wastes No Words

Mike follows a similar protocol with Lucy that he had with Gary just an hour before. He goes to her cubicle, catches her attention, and asks her to come to his office. Before they start the tandem walk down the hallway, he looks her in the eye and says, "This is going to be a very positive meeting."

It's a smart move. Mike knows that an unscheduled one-on-one with the boss is always cause for concern. A similar tap on the shoulder from Lynne would have him wondering what he was walking into. His stern initial demeanor with Gary an hour ago set the tone for that meeting. If Gary had the premonition this would be a tough sit-down with Mike, fine. If not, keeping him in suspense for the short walk down the hall wasn't a bad thing at all. The follow-up "good news" sentence to Lucy made it clear there was no reason for concern on her part.

As he did with Gary, Mike motions for Lucy to sit across from his desk and then he sits next to her. He doesn't make any small talk. He smiles and delivers his headline. "Lucy, I am promoting you to assistant manager from your supervisor's position. You'll be making more money and you're going to have more responsibility. If you're ready, let's get into the details." He tells her what her new salary would be.

"Sure, Mike, this is great news," Lucy says.

"Yes, it is, for both of us," Mike says.

3:04 Tracy Blindsides Chad

Chad returns Tracy's call on the direct line number she left and catches her at her desk immediately.

"Hi, Tracy. I didn't think we'd be speaking again so soon; but I was pleased to get your message, so I'm calling you right back. What's going on?" Chad asks.

"Chad, this call isn't about our discussions at my office this afternoon. But I will tell you, I thought we had a very pleasant and impressive meeting today, despite the fact I couldn't meet your requests. I hope you understand," Tracy says.

"Of course, Tracy. You made some good points and gave us some hope for the future," Chad responds. Since she isn't pulling back from her position, he has no idea where this is going. But he decides to stay positive.

"Listen, Chad," Tracy says, "It's not smart business to poach employees from our customers, and we know that. That's why I wanted to call you directly and ask about Randy. We have a great spot open that he would be perfect for. It's a job we think he'd find very attractive."

Chad physically pulls back from the phone while keeping the receiver to his ear. This is a real pop in the nose he didn't see coming. She wants to offer Randy a job and is calling to clear it with him. No wonder she sounded so friendly on the voice mail. She didn't have a change of heart about a deal for Chad's division at all; she wants one of his star players.

"Oh, wow, Tracy, um . . . I don't know about this at all," Chad stammers. "Randy's a pretty key cog in the wheel here."

"Listen, please don't even think about it twice then," Tracy explains. "We'll find someone else. That's exactly why I wanted to run it by you first. Randy doesn't know a thing about this; I would never approach him without asking your permission. He does a great job for you and we'd like him, but not at your expense. Congrats on having such a strong guy backing you up. We'll just let things lay then. We would never what to do anything to harm you or your company. You guys are a very valuable client for us."

She pauses for a second and then with a humorous scolding tone says, "Now that you've heard me out and we're done with that bit of business, please get Randy in high gear so he'll order more stuff from us. That way we'll get you the shipping terms and the price you want." *Tracy is sharp and clever*, Chad thinks. *She has masterfully given this touchy call an uplifting ending.*

"Well, wait just a minute, Tracy," Chad says. "I agree Randy is a tremendous asset for us. But he's a good guy, too, and I consider him a friend. Because of that I don't want to stand in his way of something that could be really good for him. Do you mind telling me what you have in mind for Randy?" Chad isn't placating Tracy. He means it. While Chad's employees find his demeanor in meetings, phone calls, and e-mails irritating and deflating most of the time, no one questions his core ethics or decency. The fact that he doesn't give Tracy a flat-out "no way" is another example of Chad's consistent sense of fair play.

At Chad's prompting, Tracy outlines the job she had in mind for Randy. She has a good read on Randy's current job and why this would be attractive. It's a definite step up for him. She wants to approach Randy about an Assistant VP position with lots of travel in the United States, as well as some international responsibilities. She hints there would probably be a nice bump in pay to boot. Randy and his wife were married less than a year ago. They have no kids, and her job as manufacturer's rep gives her plenty of leeway in her schedule. She and Randy love to travel. This job with Tracy would be a plum assignment with a strong company.

Chad's head starts to hurt again, just as it had last Friday after his 360. He is in a real bind. He doesn't want to lose Randy—a very good player for him. But he doesn't want to stand in his way. That wouldn't be right. A third and important point, he doesn't want to appear small to Tracy. Saying no to her going forward with Randy would be petty. Replacing Randy would be tough. He blurts out something direct and honest. It creates a strong connection with Tracy.

"Tracy, can you give me 'til tomorrow to go over this in my head for a few minutes? I want to do the right thing, and that means I need to play it through a few times. Can we follow up in the morning?" Chad asks.

"Of course. That's a good plan, Chad. It's what I would do." Tracy's voice is kind. "And if you decide you don't want me to pursue it with Randy, I will respect your decision, and I'll never mention it to him. This is your call all the way. That's why I'm talking to you before I ever approach Randy."

"Thanks, Tracy; and I appreciate the heads-up. This is a very classy move. You didn't have to do this. You could have just gone straight to Randy, but you called me first. That's pretty cool." Chad means it. He finds the fact he is now complimenting her on the handling of this situation quite ironic. First, this afternoon, Tracy told him directly she could not help him with the shipping or pricing thing. She also gave him a few digs along the way. Now she wants to hire away one of his best employees. Despite this, he finds he has more respect for her now than ever.

They agree to talk before lunch tomorrow. As soon as he hangs up the receiver, Chad knows he will probably give Tracy the go-ahead with Randy. He has no doubt Randy would take the offer. The job is more expansive than the one he currently has, and the pay is better. But Chad knows there is another reason Randy would jump ship. Watching Tracy in action over the last two hours, he realized she is a better boss for the upwardly mobile Randy than he is. He thinks back to his devastating 360 last Friday and realizes Tracy would have scored well on all the areas in which he received low marks.

Busted in the chops again! This is turning out to be a pretty rough day.

3:04 Mike Lays It Out for Lucy

After Mike tells Lucy she's being promoted, he goes over the reasons why. He spends the next 10 minutes going over her recent successes. He doesn't just click them off like he's reading scores or reciting a list; he methodically highlights the details of each situation. He understands the challenges she faces and what exactly she has done to help the division succeed.

"I thought we would lose the Massey–Parkland deal for sure," Mike says. "Had Louis told me they would be so unfair to us and demanding, we wouldn't even let the sales team go after it, let alone meet them on price. When you found that supplier in Belgium for us, it was a thing of beauty. Without them, we'd still be battling with those procurement guys at Perkins–Massey. Instead, the Belgium components made us look great. We completed the project, they're happy, and we made some money on it."

Lucy is delighted and surprised. The Massey–Parkland project was a royal pain in the rear for the division, but it wasn't a large order. It was more irritating than significant. Even if they had not worked things out so well, it wouldn't have made a huge impact on the P&L. Lucy had no idea that Mike had such an intimate knowledge of this one client and her role in turning a lousy situation into a victory.

And this is just one of her successes he takes the time and energy to understand. He goes through four others with the same amount of energy. Lucy is glad she is being promoted; but, more than that, she is glad she has the good fortune to work for Mike. He is direct but never abrupt. He is free and easy with compliments, and he delivers in a way that always creates a positive bounce for her.

"Okay, enough about how great you've been," Mike says with a smile. "Let's get to how you're going to be even greater, starting tomorrow." He then proceeds to lay out Lucy's new job. He goes through each new responsibility in highly specific detail. He prepared well for this meeting with Lucy.

In the past, Mike had been both happy and confused with the way his bosses had handled some of his own promotions. Several of his bosses had kept it way too short and sweet: "Mike, here's your new job. Attack it with the same skill you've demonstrated so far, and you'll keep moving up here." He'd leave promotions like that wondering what exactly was expected of him and how to get there. He vowed he'd treat every promotion for his staff the same way he'd handled the "difficult talk" with Gary just a few minutes ago. He wants Lucy to know exactly what continued success will look like and the time frame he had set for her to hit certain goals.

He explains to Lucy what is working well and what needs to be improved in each of the areas she'll be taking over. He goes through how their customers will benefit from each of his ideas. He gives her specific three-, six-, nine- and twelve-month mileposts.

Lucy is worried she doesn't have all the skills necessary to run with all of these programs. She could muddle through, of course; but she wants to do more than that. She's thirsty for more success.

Mike is ahead one step ahead of her. "You're going to be immersed in some pretty heavy customers' issues very quickly. We need to get you up to speed on some areas that will help you handle some protocols you may be a little fuzzy on," Mike says. He also tells her some technical skills he wants her to master through the headquarter's training program. He has already contacted the head of training, told her what Lucy needed, and worked out a curriculum. All Lucy has to do is make the call. She can start as soon as her schedule allows.

Then he takes a breath and looks at her. "Okay, Lucy, I've talked a lot. I need you to weigh in. Please tell me what you think."

Lucy might think this was trick question—or not a real question at all—coming from some bosses. More manipulative bosses would have deliberately left a hole in the plans or laid something out that could not be accomplished as a test. Others feigned openness, but were more interested in obedience. They would ask this question just as a courtesy. But Mike doesn't play games, and he isn't controlling. He asked for her opinion of his plan because he wants them to come to a strong agreement. She begins to go through his ideas step by step.

3:15 Chad Lays It On Way Too Thick

DeShawn shows up at Chad's door right on time. Chad, all smiles, stays seated and waves him in, motioning for him to sit down across from him.

"Hey, DeShawn, thanks for coming in." Chad is chipper. He has given himself a stern talking to and is determined to put on his game face, despite the repeated body slams today. When the going gets tough, the tough get going, he says, forgetting for the moment who coined the phrase. No matter; it was quite applicable, especially today.

"Sure thing, Chad. What's up?" DeShawn responds. He, like all of Chad's employees, has accepted that Chad's insincere meeting rhetoric was just part of the job. What he's thinking is, *like I had a choice. You sent me an e-mail last week, asking me to meet with you in your office at 3:15. Since I work for you, and you can see my whole calendar on our system, I didn't really have very many options on this, did I?* DeShawn doesn't find Chad offensive—just not very helpful.

"Well, I want you to know that I love your attitude around here. You take on every challenge with gusto, and, most of the time, you succeed. And even when you don't, you bust your rear end trying. You're the type of 'can do' person we need to propel us forward," Chad leans forward, interlocking his fingers. He shakes his one giant first in rhythm with his words.

"But, I'm sure I'm not telling you anything you don't already know," Chad finishes.

DeShawn hopes he isn't confused. From Chad's sloppy compliments and weird finish, it isn't clear whether he is asking DeShawn if he knows he is appreciated, or if DeShawn thinks highly of himself. It wouldn't be very humble to give a yes to either. So he decides to play it down the middle.

"I'm glad you're pleased with my work, Chad. I like it here." That's true. DeShawn does enjoy the job, the division, and the goals of the larger company. He can live with the fact that Chad, despite his quick mind and professional look, acts like a sitcom character.

Chad unclasps his hands and uses a toss-off motion with one of them, "Oh please, don't be so modest. You are a real star here, and it's about time we start treating you like one." As the words come out of his mouth, Chad realizes DeShawn might find them a little insincere, but he can't help himself.

Chad is feeling very insecure over all the events of the day, especially Tracy's play for Randy. To overcompensate, he keeps heaping broad praise on DeShawn.

Finally, he gets to the point. He explains to DeShawn what his new title and position will be. Chad also provides some broad strokes on the new areas of responsibility. He steers clear of setting any specific goals and objectives for DeShawn. *No use in going through nitty-gritty stuff when you reward someone for their hard work with a promotion*, thinks Chad. Last, Chad tells

DeShawn about the raise in pay, with a bit too much paternal affection in his voice. That along with his overly broad smile clearly pose the rhetorical question: I'm a prince of a boss, now aren't I?

DeShawn says all the right things in response. He's happy for the promotion and the raise. He doesn't mention that he has some trepidation about what the new post will bring in terms of specific project expectations, since Chad didn't give him too many details. But he realizes that this was all Chad wants to tell him right now, and he isn't going to complain about it.

They shake hands, and Chad attempts to add a little extra intensity to the parting by patting DeShawn on the shoulder. It isn't creepy or anything; but it isn't effective, either. DeShawn feels pretty good, but not fired up.

Chad felt wonderful. *Finally, something went according to plan,* he thinks.

3:32 Mike Writes a Personal Note

Lucy went into specifics quickly about needs in her department, and how quickly those changes could be implemented. Mike listens and asks questions but doesn't agree to implement any of them. Instead, they have a spirited discussion about the issues, which they agree to revisit in a month. She knows that he takes her ideas seriously. It's obvious to her that he has thought about how she fits into the team, and specifically how her talents can be used.

Wow, a better title, a bigger paycheck, more training, and Mike's ear for the better part of an hour. That's a heck of good meeting for her. What she doesn't know is that she's going to get a call from her parents a week later, telling her that they have received a letter from Mike, congratulating them on her success and spelling out the reasons for her promotion.

3:00 PM

Don't Be That Boss Lessons

3:01 Chad Perceives a Silver Lining

✓ A small measure of paranoia is good for all bosses. Don't congratulate yourself too quickly without assessing possible downsides.

3:02 Mike Wastes No Words

✓ With good news as well as with bad news, get to the headlines quickly.

3:04 Tracy Blindsides Chad

✓ Poor communicators will lose great employees to strong communicators.

3:04 Mike Lays It Out for Lucy

✓ Employees understand promotions are best when they are described in rich detail about future assignments instead of just filled with praise.

(*continued*)

(*continued*)

3:15 Chad Lays It On Way Too Thick

✓ Broad praise is never helpful for employees or bosses. When you go into specifics to back up your commendation, you create stronger connections with employees.

3:32 Mike Writes a Personal Note

✓ A promotion meeting is a great opportunity to exchange ideas and set new goals. Great bosses move past the new title and pay quickly to discuss deeper issues in the organization.

4:00 PM

Chad's Production Meeting: Just the Facts, Ma'am

4:01 Chad Relinquishes Some Power

The production team is seated around the table in the big conference room, with Chad, as usual, seated at the head and Randy next to him. Mike comes in, moves a free chair away from the table, and settles in at the back of the room across the table from Chad and Randy.

"Mike's here to take a gander at how we do things at our end of the hall," Chad explains. This doesn't raise an eyebrow for the production team. Everyone knows Mike and Chad are buddies and like to exchange notes frequently. "Mike, please jump in to lend a hand or ask a question, if you feel the urge." Mike just nods. Per a previous agreement with Chad, Mike will just observe. He'll have no speaking role in the meeting.

"Well, Randy, why don't we make this your rodeo for the day?" Chad turns to Randy. "Go ahead and take control." This is a complete surprise to everyone sitting around the table, especially Randy. Chad isn't only the boss of the division; he makes himself the boss of every meeting as well. Production is no exception.

Chad hadn't planned on any change of plans until he saw Mike coming in the door of the conference room just a moment before. That—coupled with the realization that he would be giving Tracy the go-ahead to approach Randy tomorrow—caused him to abruptly change the protocol and decide to make Randy the boss for the meeting. He'd look munificent to Mike and maybe show Randy how much he was appreciated in the process. Chad is proud of his flexibility in seizing a nice leadership opportunity.

While Randy is happy to lead the meeting, he wonders why Chad didn't give him a bit more warning. He doesn't flinch at the task; but he doesn't feel especially appreciated, either. *Just another taste of Chad-style leadership from the hip*, Randy thinks. He looks down at the reports and clears his throat, "Thanks, Chad. Okay then, let's get going."

"Unless somebody's got a crash and burn anywhere, let's start with Whitney. What did we move out the door this week?" Chad turns to Whitney and looks down to focus on the shipping stats, which are on the second page of the production report.

4:06 Balancing Customer Demands with Profit Margin

"Well, actually, I do have a touchy situation I need to bring up," Simone interrupts. "It's not a crash and burn, but I've got to figure out how to handle something that's just come up with Rob Nicholson about 20 minutes ago. We need to go over it now, if we can."

Chad's back stiffens. This isn't good. He keeps silent, which is a struggle.

Simone explains that their customer, Rob Nicholson, called this morning and politely but firmly requested shipment of his order two weeks early. Rob told Simone it wasn't his fault or some mismanaged calculation. His customer had suddenly pushed his delivery date forward, and so he had to push Simone. There was just no way around it.

Chad hates this "customer basket case" scenario. He had spent hours in the last year streamlining his production process, measuring every minute of labor along with each dollar of materials along the way. He knows *exactly* what his costs are. As a result, on most projects, the gross margins for his division are good. The capable Randy rides herd on production expenses. When a customer asks for preferential shipping treatment—as Rob Nicholson was now doing—it screws everything up. There's no leeway for this type of thing in the lean production models Chad has created. The meltdown and late shipments that had bothered Steve Moreno so much were indeed rare. The perfect storm analogy was perfectly accurate; it just wasn't helpful in the discussions with Steve.

Chad can stay quiet no longer. He's heard enough. "You've got to explain to Rob that this just isn't going to work for us. He'll have to understand and make adjustments from his end. His lack of planning or proper management of his customers shouldn't make for an emergency for us," Chad blurts out, taking control of the meeting from Randy.

Simone is uncomfortable. She disagrees with Chad on two fronts. First, it isn't fair. Rob explained to her in great detail the bind he was in, and he made good sense. He didn't ask for favors like this very often and he was right to want to keep his customers happy. Second, Rob is the head of procurement for his firm. He makes the buying decisions. Simone knows that he likes working with Chad's division, but if she tells him off using any of Chad's words, he'll go elsewhere. There are companies other than Chad's division that could help him, and they are lucky to have Rob as a customer.

"I'm sorry, Chad, but that's just not going to work very well for us in this instance," Simone says. Nobody actually gasps audibly, but there is some minor drama in the room. Chad's staff just does not stand up to him openly in any meeting—let alone with an outsider like Mike in the room. Chad simply doesn't allow that type of direct debate once he weighs in. Instead, his managers shrug, tacitly agree, and then work around it later behind his back. Or they spend a lot of time in separate one-on-one meetings with Chad working on him to change his mind, which he often will. It's all a huge waste of time, they think, but it's how Chad runs things.

But here was Simone, throwing down in front of everybody—including Mike.

First Phil this morning, now Simone, thinks Chad. *Why am I cursed with people who won't follow simple directions they agree to? What has gotten into everybody?*

4:13 Simone Stands Strong . . . for a While

"Okay, fine, whatever," says Chad. "But let's give ourselves some breathing room on this thing. Make no hard-and-fast commitment, Simone. When you talk to him, tell him we'll do everything we can to meet his request . . . that we'll do our very best for him, but don't make any promises until Randy and I take a look at how we can salvage margin out of this project. Just be vague."

"Chad, I apologize for disagreeing again, but Rob doesn't care how hard we'll try to meet his request. He needs a yes or no answer when I call him in a few minutes. He's way too sharp to be manipulated. Being squishy won't work with this guy. I'd rather tell him we can't meet his deadline than lead him on, only to disappoint him if we can't make the numbers work."

The mild drama has shifted to out-and-out tension. Simone isn't backing down an inch. No one has seen this before. Chad studies his report for a minute. He raises his head and glares at Simone.

"Then you tell Rob Nicholson we're not going to do it. He can't say 'jump' when he wants and we just ask 'how high.' If we let all our customers do that, we'd start to go out of business. Our production protocols are important. We can't mess with them. He'll just have to understand. We can't help him," Chad says, turning to everyone in the room with the slow pronouncement.

"Fine, Chad, on your directive, that's what I'll do," Simone says, unsuccessfully concealing the facetiousness in her voice. It isn't fine at all. She wants to meet Rob's request. She is severely disappointed in Chad's lack of flexibility and shortsightedness with a good customer. *What good is manically controlling your costs if you're going to chase good customers away and your revenue drops?* she wonders.

Randy breaks the silence. "Hey, Simone—how about this as an alternative? Do you think Rob can cough up some extra budget dollars in exchange for us expediting the process? I'm not talking about a big penalty—just 3 or 4 percent so we don't lose that much money with the extra work and disruption inefficiencies we'll have deal with."

"I don't know," says Simone, "but I like that tactic a lot better than a flat-out 'we can't help you.' This gives him a 'yes' and then he can decide whether or not to spend the extra money to get what he needs. This might work out well for everybody. It's worth a shot. I'm on board with that."

Chad calculates quickly and sees Randy's idea still won't remedy the situation financially. "Randy, you know how much a production schedule change costs us. We're still way behind the eight ball even with the 3 or 4 percent. He should pay at least a 12 percent penalty for screwing up our lives. Even at that, we're still not operating the way we should."

Randy admits Chad is right. Charging 3 or 4 percent is not enough. But he felt it was a reasonable request—something Simone could get behind and Rob would probably agree to. He decides to push back on Chad. "There's no way Rob's going to go for a 10 or 12 percent increase. He'll say we're holding his order hostage. He'll start looking for another supplier, which he'll be able to find. Let's give Simone some leeway on this, and see if she can get some money out of Rob for us and still make him happy."

"Hey, Randy, it's your meeting. You're calling the shots here. I was just trying to make a point, that's all," Chad says. "Once you start letting your customers run your operation, you start having real trouble. You'll all see when we get the final job costs on this one that we won't make as much as we should have. But if that's how you want to handle it, go right ahead. I won't complain." He knows it's wrong in principle; but he caves on purpose. He wants to make an obvious show of magnanimity. Chad is happy to play the great guy, but frustrated that they can't do the math the way he can. A 3 or 4 percent bump is a lousy compromise.

No one in that room, including Randy, would have used the words "great guy" to describe Chad after what had just occurred. "Petulant child," sure; but "great guy," no way.

"Okay, Simone, let's go forward with this. I know you need to duck out and call Rob. Come back and let us know how it went, if we're still in the room when you wrap up with him," says Randy.

Simone grabs her report, calendar, and BlackBerry, and dashes out of the room.

4:28 Randy Changes the Routine

"Whitney," Randy says. "Now, it's your turn. Tell us about what we've wrapped up in the last week."

Whitney is the final member of Chad's production team to touch each project as it is handed over to the client. During these meetings her role is to go over the five to ten projects that have been wrapped up in the last week. This morning, with the heavy air in the room, she tries to run through them quickly.

But Randy slows down her pace, asking her about several of her final meetings and discussions with customers. Then he comes up with a question Chad would never ask.

"Whitney, tell us how you think this customer would grade our performance on this project," he asks. Randy, Chad, and the rest of the team usually have a broad picture of what's going out the door, but Whitney is the one who gets the final read from customers on each job, and even more so than individual project managers.

Chad doesn't like where Randy was going with this, but he succeeds in keeping quiet. However, most of the production team members immediately notice a shift in his posture that indicates his displeasure. *What a waste of time*, Chad thinks. *Whitney doesn't have a lot of technical expertise and is just a click or two above a clerical employee. Why is Randy bothering to ask her, when I've hired the best consultant in the country to conduct customer satisfaction surveys? Whatever we'll hear from her isn't as professional or statistically valid as what the consultant's report will tell us at the end of the year.*

Whitney, however, is pleased to answer Randy's unexpected questions. Chad never talks to Whitney directly unless there is a blowup with a customer long after delivery. Or he might go back and check with her on some items when a customer decided to competitively bid out a project that Chad was sure the division had in the bag already.

So, she shares two stories: a positive story from a customer and then a lackluster one. They're both small issues that didn't cause a significantly beneficial or harmful ripple, but still they catch the interest of everyone in the room. The customers see Whitney as someone who had a more sympathetic ear to their issues than the individual project managers, who are always under pressure from Chad to meet the numbers. They often confide in her about minor bumps and snags about the process that they would hesitate to bring up in formal customer-vendor production meetings.

Randy feels Whitney adds great value for the production team beyond her actual duties. Customers open up to Whitney. He sees her as a strong, underutilized part of the team. Additionally, the other project managers like the extra time that Randy is spending with Whitney. Hearing her insights every week would help them perform better, because they want to know what the customers are thinking as well—even about small items.

Chad is delighted at his self-restraint as he allows Randy to proceed with this discussion unfettered—despite the fact that he considers the discussion a complete waste of time. Customers always whine a little, usually in an effort to get a better price next time. *As long as we deliver what we said we would, when we said we would, what else is there, really?*

Chad politely asks Randy if he can ask a few questions. Randy of course agrees, and then Chad weighs in. No one in the room is surprised at the questions, which all pertain to gross margin, final vendor's costs, and early projected profit. Chad loves the numbers; they tell him everything he needs to know.

4:39 Back to the Regular Routine

Now it's time for the project managers to report. By Chad's directive, they have filled out and e-mailed a detailed spreadsheet to Randy by the previous Friday afternoon. Randy then collated the reports electronically into a single page that provides a quick glimpse of the breakdown for each project.

The project managers reel off their reports one by one, reading what is on the spreadsheet. Randy decides he's upset the apple cart plenty for one day so he's content just to let this part of the meeting flow as usual. The project managers go through the play-by-play, but Chad provides the commentary. When the numbers are subpar, Chad—as he does every week—adds one or two words of criticism like, "unacceptable," "poor planning," or even the sarcastic "well, congrats to this client for digging so consistently and successfully into our pockets." To

drive home the point, Chad has fixed the spreadsheet software to create a bright red border around every number that is
off plan.

Everyone in the room has the intellect and the experience
to understand what makes for a poor production report number.
But no one on the team, except perhaps Randy, knows what
exactly they might do to improve the poor production number.
Despite that, Chad likes to repeat the slogans for success that
they hear every week: "work harder," or "negotiate better," or
his favorite, "understand that failure is not an option here." Even
though he asks few questions, there's no doubt in the room about
what Chad determines a success. If someone makes a particularly
good buy with a vendor or manages their hours for the week
well on a specific project, he'll pipe in with "excellent," or "that's
how it's done. . .we need this type of performance every week
on every project."

Chad rarely asks about the clients during the project
report—and today is no exception. If the discussion veers too
much toward customers' issues and concerns, as it had with
Simone, Chad listens for a minute or two and then cuts it
off once he understands the financial implications. He thinks
too many production people fret too much about what clients
think. *We need to worry about ourselves, not them*, he believes. *Give
them the good value we agreed upon. If they complain too loud, or
if we screw up, throw them a bone; but stop wasting time yammering
about it.*

4:47 Simone Comes Back with a Win

Chad usually ends the meeting with what he thinks is a great
flourish by giving his team a letter grade for the week. Chad is

proud of the letter grade moment and believes everyone is on the edge of their chair wondering what score he'll give.

As Randy is starting the wrap-up after the final project report, Simone pops back in the room. She is smiling. "He said he could authorize another 3 percent for us, and he's very appreciative we can meet his time frame. We're good with him." She is obviously pleased with the Rob Nicholson results.

The room becomes buoyant for a few moments with the news. It's a nice story of success and everyone feels a part of it. "Good job, Simone. Well, everybody, we'll see you next week," Randy says.

Everyone starts to gather their BlackBerrys and notepads. Chad leans over to Randy and whispered, "What, no letter grade?" Randy responds sheepishly, "Oh, sorry, must have forgotten with Simone's good news and all. But that's for you to dispense, not me. I'll do it the next time you have me run a meeting, if you like, but I don't want to just copy you. You're the boss and the one who should give a grade."

Randy is lying. He hates the letter grade and finds it patronizing. He omitted it on purpose and would not do it again next time, if ever, Chad coughed up the meeting to him.

4:55 Mike Asks for Chad to Return the Favor

Mike stays in the room until everyone left. Chad says, "Well, what have you got for me? That was some display of chutzpah from Simone, huh? But what are you going to do? Even good people just don't get it sometimes. Anyway, I'm dying to hear what you think."

"What I think is that I'd like to really take full advantage of some of the things you are doing. My mind was racing as I sat in on your meeting. I see a lot that would help me, and I've got some ideas for you. I know it's last minute, but how about you coming to my production meeting right now—and then we compare notes after work together? I want your help as well."

The tight-ship Chad always scheduled a free hour from 5 PM to 6 PM to clean up loose details and prepare for the next day. But he wanted to know what Mike had to say, and he was interested to see how the other group's meeting ran compared to his own.

"Yeah, good idea. I can do it. I'll clean up a few things on my desk and slip in right as you guys are starting."

4:00 PM

Don't Be That Boss Lessons

4:01 Chad Relinquishes Some Power

✓ If you are going to give employees the spotlight, make sure they are aware of their new responsibilities ahead of time so that they can make the most of the opportunity.

4:06 Balancing Customer Demands with Profit Margin

✓ Remember that our customers provide the money that allows us to remain in business. Always take full measure of a customer's requests for change of scope or delivery time, and try to find a middle ground.

(continued)

(*continued*)

4:13 Simone Stands Strong ... for a while

✓ Listen to employees' arguments carefully and never summarily dismiss them—especially in front of other team members.

4:28 Randy Changes the Routine

✓ Take advantage of the wide variety of ways in which your customers will communicate their satisfaction with your performance for them.

4:39 Back to the Regular Routine

✓ Employees cannot improve performance of their key indicators unless they can see and understand what successful behavior looks like.

4:47 Simone Comes Back with a Win

✓ Letter grades and numeric performance evaluation only take on meaning when they are reinforced with specific details of success and failure.

4:55 Mike Asks for Chad to Return the Favor

✓ Good bosses are always seeking to gain greater insight into ways they can improve their own performance.

5:00 PM
Mike's
Production
Meeting:
Not Exactly Kumbaya, but Lots of Give-and-Take

5:02 Chad Receives a Warm Welcome

Chad is still fuming about Simone's open insubordination as he walks down the hall to Mike's conference room. As usual, at about this time he's carrying around a water bottle containing a thick, fuchsia-colored liquid—water mixed with protein energy powder that he got from his nutritionist. Chad likes the little boost the organic mixture gives him at the end of the day. He

175

believes it helps him squeeze a little bit of extra productivity out of the five to six o'clock hour.

"Hey, you'll spoil your dinner with those empty calories," he says to Mike, who was holding half a donut covered with powdered sugar. They meet up right outside of the conference room, where Mike's team members are milling around and chatting.

"You know, a petrified stale sugar donut is just the bit of nutrition I need to power through an end-of-the-day production meeting. Besides, even a little stale, I'll bet it's tastier than what you're downing. What is that anyway? It looks like Clairol Herbal Essence," Mike teases.

"Well, it cleans out my pores. Listen, you need to get more of that donut into your mouth next time," Chad replies, flicking his index finger dramatically up and down on his own upper lip.

"Thanks, buddy," Mike says, wiping his mouth with the paper napkin he's been using to hold the donut. "And now that you've gone out of the way to point it out, I can see you do have pretty doggone good pores."

"Damn right I do," Chad agrees as they open the glass door and walk into the conference room.

"Okay, Kim, sorry for not giving you any warning on this, but we have a guest in our meeting," Mike says. "I've asked Chad to sit in with us, see what we do, and give me some pointers. Kim, you have my permission to make Chad feel like one of our own."

Kim, Mike's boss of production, quickly picks up the cue. "Alright everybody, you heard the man, assume the position," Kim barks. Everyone around the table holds their hands, poised in clapping mode, up for Kim to see.

"Okay, Chad, welcome to our production meeting," Kim announces and nods. All hands came together lightly, bestowing the golf clap of appreciation upon Chad. Kim stole the idea from Louis, who ran sales for Mike. Her team embraced the clever recognition exercise.

Chad, a first time recipient, likes it, too, as he smiles and waves his hand to everyone. But as soon as it's over, he worries they aren't showing enough respect to a division manager. *Are they giving it to me a little bit, or do I just need to get over myself?* he wonders.

"What a great way to start a meeting at the end of the day," Kim says. "Let's move through the good-news, bad-news portion, and then we'll do the detailed thing." She looks directly at Mike. She is hoping he will acknowledge that she started the meeting as instructed, without the usual "Okay, people."

Mike noticed. He smiles and gives her a slight "well done" nod.

5:05 Lots of Great Info, but No Numbers

"Jake, you're up," Kim says, motioning to the man to her right.

"A bit of both today," Jake says. "Hearthstone thinks we walk on water. They've got two more things for us at the end of the year. Mike, I've already e-mailed Louis about it. On the negative side . . . we'll, it's not really negative, but it's not exactly positive, so I want you to know about it. Holland Resources is not very excited about the first set of design specs that we came up with. But I'll have more on that later."

"Good. Okay, Leslie, your turn," Kim says, nodding to the woman next to Jake.

"It's all good. We had three go out the door last week to cheery customers—on time, and the numbers look pretty good, too. The guys at FQA took the whole team out for a bite and even picked up the check," Leslie says. "I'm sure Rebecca here has equally good news to share."

The room explodes with laughter while Rebecca shakes her head. "Thanks, Leslie. This is just what I need at the end of the day," Rebecca says. "As Kim can attest, we are not in good shape with Oakmont Data at all. We've made little or no progress since the first meeting six weeks ago. I'm amazed these guys can make money when they're at each other's throats so much."

There are knowing nods around the room. The Oakmont management team is very contentious with each other—and with Rebecca as well. As soon as she'd get a situation straight with one VP, another Oakmont VP would step in and create havoc. Mike's whole division had heard about the mess, and the other project managers provided lots of empathy. They'd all had one or two clients from hell and knew how trying it could be.

"Kim, we might have to bring Mike in on this if I don't make some headway pretty soon," Rebecca finishes.

Mike doesn't wait for Kim to answer. "Well, we'll see," he says directly.

Chad found that he could not process quickly enough everything he had just seen. They were already 10 minutes into the meeting; and he realized that he had a very good feel for what was going on in Mike's division. That was . . . well, weird because there was no report to analyze, no spreadsheets, no quantitative data. Everyone was just going from their own mental notes and simply discussing customer reactions to the work of Mike's production team.

On top of that, he's shocked that Mike would allow the project managers in the room to be so cavalier with regard to Rebecca's major issues with Oakmont. No progress in six weeks means that this project is seriously in trouble and already costing Mike considerable margin dollars. That is never something to joke about. Everyone in the division obviously knows the trouble at Oakmont, because of the laughs Leslie got when she baited Rebecca. The openness with which Mike's project managers share good as well as bad news is confusing to Chad. They are freely admitting failures—and even anticipating future ones—without having hard data to trigger defensive discussions of poor performance.

Finally, Mike himself surprised Chad. He thought when Rebecca reached out and mentioned that she might need his help, great guy Mike would jump right in with encouraging words. In fact, it was quite the opposite; he was outwardly standoffish. He didn't even commit to helping Kim and Rebecca with the jerks at Oakmont. Why on earth would he say, "We'll see," when they obviously needed his help? Wasn't it the boss's job to jump in and help solve problems? Did Mike not like or respect Rebecca, and so was dismissing her? Also, he didn't offer an "attaboy" to Jake for his great success or to Leslie for her home runs, either. He just sat and listened, not cheering good news or showing concern over bad news. *I'd never have that kind of restraint,* Chad thinks. *How does he do it? More important—why does he do it?*

Chad is conflicted; but he is glad to be the fly on the wall this time.

5:15 Leslie Explains Why a Chore She Dislikes Has Helped Her

Kim continues to shepherd the good-news/bad-news report around the table. Chad is able to figure out that, overall, Mike's production team is doing well. The only glaring issue is the situation with Oakmont.

"Good job, everyone, now on to the meat of the matter. Leslie, I think it's your turn this week."

"That's right, Kim. I'm starting to get the hang of this, after several turns now. I got it all done this time in less than an hour," Leslie says as she starts to hand out stapled production reports around the room.

"Hey, Kim—why don't you give Chad a heads-up as to what's going on right now?" Mike asks. He wants Chad to understand how his team developed their report. It's the main reason he had asked Chad to join in the meeting; he wants Chad's help to make this report a better tool for the team.

"Sure, Mike. Chad, every week a different program manager is responsible for pulling together our production data. That means that, every six weeks or so, these guys get out of their own little worlds and have to pull labor and materials information about what's going on with every project in the division to format the report. Nobody loves doing it; but switching around gives all of us stronger insight into what's really going on with everyone else."

"Hey, Mike, can I ask a follow-up question to Kim?" Chad says.

"Sure, please do," Mike says.

"Wouldn't it be more efficient if just one of you were responsible for this report—the one with the best software skills? I can see that there's a lot of stuff here. If you have to rotate, with one of you doing it once only every six weeks, you're not going to be as fast as if just one of you, well, kind of mastered the thing and made it your own baby," Chad says.

"Chad is right! And I think he should come to our meetings more often," Leslie blurts out. Once again, there is laughter all around, the loudest from Leslie herself.

"Okay, Leslie, explain to Chad why we do it this way," Kim says.

"Well, all right then," Leslie says slowly, as if she were a child being told to eat her vegetables. Then she perks up and plays it straight. "Chad, at first I didn't like doing the reports. I found them to be a real struggle for exactly the reasons you spelled out. In fact, several months ago, I voiced my concerns and volunteered Jake here, the data guru, to handle this for us. He's better at it and can pull everything together in a third of the time that any one of us can. I was overruled, though—not by Jake, but by everyone else.

"And here's why: Even though it's a pain in the butt, I get to see what every other project is really delivering to our division at least once every six weeks. Creating the report takes a lot more concentration than just listening to the numbers and discussions in the meeting for a half an hour a week—which is what you're going to see happen in the next half hour," Leslie continues.

"When it's my dreaded turn, I can see how the numbers for each project change and move, based on decisions Jake, Rebecca, Kim, or anyone else involved in production will make." Leslie turns to Chad for emphasis. "So even though I'm not a fan of taking the time to put this together, I've learned a lot doing it. I have found myself asking questions of the other project managers I never would have without having to put the numbers to these golden templates." Leslie smiles. "And now I can do it in a lot less than three hours. How about some love, huh?"

"She's right," says Kim. "Assume the position. And go!"

Leslie beams at being the recipient of the golf clap, even though she had to beg for it.

Kim turns to Chad. "Does that give you what you need, Chad, or would you like for us to go further into this?"

"No, no, this is great. Thanks for the explanation," Chad says.

5:30 Rebecca Needs to Work Harder

Everyone in the room has already flipped through copies of Leslie's report. They are now ready to discuss their projects in detail.

"Okay, problem child, you first," Kim says to Rebecca.

"Gladly. I really need some help on this one," Rebecca says.

Chad can see from the page on the production report dedicated to the Oakmont project that he was right about Mike being underwater already on this one. The report has about five key indicators, matching budgeting time and materials to actual costs during each phase of production. Rebecca is still in the planning and design stage and way over on her labor hours. This is the type of analysis at which Chad excels. In seconds, he calculates they wouldn't even break even on this unless they could catch up and right the ship quickly.

Chad can also see the report is pretty thin in terms of detail. There are a few more subcategories that Mike could easily add to this template that would give him and everyone else a lot more insight into how the project is proceeding. Chad makes a note on his copy of the production report to mention it later to Mike in their mutual debriefing. As usual, he is happy to help.

"My problem with Oakmont is that it's a case of one step forward, and two steps back," explains Rebecca. "I can't ever get all the partners—or at least the critical ones—at the same meeting, even though I make sure all the key players receive the same urgent e-mails. I mean, they *are* paying us money, aren't they? Why are they deliberately sabotaging us by not holding each other accountable to show up to meetings?" Rebecca is clearly frustrated.

Kim jumps in, "Yeah, she's right. I've seen it in person. The partners that show up give us pretty strong direction and we think, 'well, we're starting to move now.' Later, sometimes the same day, we get e-mails and calls from the absent partners telling us the other guys got it all wrong and that we need to go in another direction. It's a real cluster, every time. I don't know what to do. Any ideas, anyone?"

"Yeah, I have a question," asks Ronnie, another production manager. "What do they think about us? I mean, I hope they aren't blaming us when they can't get their own act together."

"Well, we're the one thing they can agree on," says Rebecca. "They think this start/stop/start process is mostly our fault. I can't imagine *why* they think that; but 'fault' is the word they use, and they lay it on us every time we have another do-over with them."

A few in the room exhale; others look down, pondering where to go with this tough one. Rebecca is a strong project manager. Her clients and her team like her, and she is always direct about her wins and losses. "You can tell from the report I'm over my labor by 26 percent already just in the planning and design stage. This is going to be a financial train wreck."

Chad can see the others are quietly struggling to come up with ideas to help Rebecca. He doesn't have any easy answers, either. This Oakmont thing is a mess in every way. He wonders how Mike is going to handle the situation.

Kim breaks the silence. "Hey, Mike, how do you feel about taking a trip out there with us? From my vantage point, it looks like we could use you now."

"I'm not ready to dive in with them yet," Mike says. "Kim, can I go ahead and ask some questions to get some clarity?"

"Yeah, of course," says Kim. Chad wonders why Mike would even ask for permission. This is his team. He should ask questions whenever he damn well pleases.

"Rebecca, are the partners at Oakmont pretty sharp? I mean—they have plenty of strong intellect, don't they?" Mike asks.

"Yeah, of course; they're all brainiacs. That's the problem, maybe," Rebecca answers.

"And you're positive they got the e-mail invites to the meetings, right?"

"Yeah, sure. They all accept every invite, sometimes with comments saying that they're looking forward to attending," Rebecca says, slowly. She is picking up where Mike is going with this. It isn't going to be positive for her.

"Then why aren't they showing up, Rebecca?" Mike asked.

Rebecca knows the answer—and so does everyone else in the room except Chad. "The Oakmont guys aren't coming to the meetings because they think they don't have to," she says, starting to look down at the table in front of her. Mike is leading her to the conclusion that she has to first shoulder the blame for this.

"Okay, good. Now that we've got that straight—what are you going to do next?" Mike asked. He isn't smiling.

Mike has told all of his teammates repeatedly of his belief that everyone—vendors, customers, employees—does what they think they *have* to do. If you spend time and energy describing vivid details of positive results when someone does what you want—as well as the same type of vivid details of negative results if they don't—then your chances of success increase. Everyone in the room, especially Kim, has experienced the "people do what they think they have to" lecture from Mike more than once.

"Well, I'm going to work hard to explain to all of them—in one-on-one conversations on the phone if I have to—what success looks like if they show up and what failure looks like if they don't," Rebecca says. She goes on to describe a few of the positive scenarios if they get their act together—and some negative ones if they don't. The group helps her pick the best ones. She looks more optimistic and tells the group she will start on the process tomorrow.

Mike turns to Kim, "So it doesn't look like I have to make a trip to Oakmont yet, does it?" He is giving her some criticism, right in front of the others, Chad realizes. She called on his help too early. This is something she should have been on top of. Kim looks right at him and says, "You're right." Mike nods.

5:40 Chad Thought He'd See More Backslapping

"Okay Ronnie, you're next," Kim says. The Oakmont quandary is over. Rebecca took the blame for the lousy performance and came up with a new tactic, to which everyone in the group contributed. It was a good outcome.

And so Kim continues to go around the room; and she turns to Mike to ask questions frequently. Chad notices that Mike challenges his production people much more than he does. Mike doesn't accept brief or glib responses to his questions; he digs and digs until he understands the *true* bottom line and the meat of what is really going on with each project. Chad can see that the probing always results in some type of minor—and occasionally major—production or customer service revelation, with the results helping everyone.

When these successes occur, Mike claps his hands and almost shouts: "If you were a five-hundred-dollar-an-hour 'best practices consultant,' you would have just earned a day's worth of pay. Well done!" This bit of good-natured sarcasm is a real compliment and warrants a golf clap from everyone.

Mike hates what he calls "MBA nano-speak." No one in his production team—or in his entire division, for that matter—is allowed to use the phrases "best practices," "matrix driven organization," "thinking outside the box," or "picking the low-hanging fruit." He coaches his employees at all levels to be direct, paint a picture of success or failure when trying to make a point, and devote energy to their communication efforts. It pays off.

Occasionally, Mike asks Kim to slow down a bit as they go over the percentages of completion numbers and projected gross margins. Everyone knows that grasping the numbers—especially financial stats—isn't Mike's strong suit. But Chad can see that this doesn't diminish Mike's leadership strength. He has surrounded himself with people who are math and engineering wizards, and they're always around to help him out.

Chad can see that he and Mike run their production meetings and overall departments much differently. Mike's entire focus is on customer benchmarks and deadlines. He spends a lot of time exploring whether his production staff is creating a positive customer experience. It's now obvious to Chad that Mike sees production excellence and sales volume as being intertwined—not as separate functions within the division.

But that's not the real "aha" for Chad. He's never really seen Mike in action like this. Chad thought Mike got his great results from exemplifying Mr. Charming—always the one with the perfect words for every situation. Now he can see that Mike's words can be specifically critical at times when they need to be. Mike produces great results from his team, but exhibits very tough, consistent, and nurturing leadership along the way.

Chad can't figure out how Mike can pull off being tough and kind at the same time. But he can't wait to find out.

5:00 PM

Don't Be That Boss Lessons

5:02 Chad Receives a Warm Welcome

✓ Bosses need input from other bosses whom they respect in order to succeed. A strong peer will give you insight that your employees—and even your own boss—won't.

5:05 Lots of Great Info, but No Numbers

✓ Push your employees to lead using descriptive headlines, instead of numbers, when discussing production issues.

(continued)

(continued)

5:15 Leslie Explains Why a Chore She Dislikes Has Helped Her

✓ Employees should often take on chores that are not in their primary skill set to gain greater knowledge of how to best succeed in your operation.

5:30 Rebecca Needs to Work Harder

✓ Don't allow your employees to blame customers easily or quickly for production miscues.

5:40 Chad Thought He'd See More Backslapping

✓ You can coach employees more effectively by listening and probing with questions than just offering advice and solutions.

6:00 PM
AFTER WORK
DOWNTIME:
Mike and Chad
Hash It Out

6:01 Chad Loosens Up

Mike and Chad are standing in the reception area all packed up and ready to go—coats on and valises in hand. They're both throwing out ideas about the best place to have an after-work drink, when Mike's controller Ellen walks up. She's also heading out the door on her way home.

"Wow, this looks like a heavy discussion," she jokes.

"Why, yes, Ellen; trying to maximize ambiance while imbibing is important," Mike says.

"Well, I'm sure you'll figure it out when you get thirsty enough," she says, nodding at Chad. She reaches for the office door.

"Hey, Ellen, one quick question, if you don't mind," Mike says. He has a very straight face.

"Yes, Mike . . . of course." She squares up to look at both of them. This is going to take a minute. She obviously doesn't mind.

"Well, I just wanted to know, what happens *'when a problem comes along'*?"

Chad has no idea what Mike is talking about.

"Oh, Mike, for gosh sakes, you really aren't working very hard are you?" Ellen questions. "Well, *'when a problem comes along, you must whip it.'*"

"*Whip it?*" Mike asks, smiling.

"Yes, Mike, *whip it good*. I have to go now," Ellen is still in character.

"Yeah, Mike, let her go home, *before the cream sits out too long*," Chad blurts out. He surprises himself—and them. He can't believe he just joined in their little lyrics game.

Ellen laughs out loud. Mike drops his valise to the ground and pounds Chad on the back. "Well done, my friend. We'll have to include you in the reindeer games more often."

Ellen says good-bye and walked out. Mike and Chad agree to meet up in a sports bar in a hotel outside of downtown. Since there aren't any games on this early, there probably won't be much of a crowd.

6:15 Mike Starts In

Mike and Chad grab a booth at the back of the bar. They have made a good choice. It is quiet, and the server is happy to see some customers.

"What can I get you guys tonight?" she asks.

"What kind of nonalcoholic beers do you have?" Chad asks. He picks one of the two she offered, and Mike orders a regular draft.

"You on the wagon or something?" Mike asks.

"Not at all; but I never drink unless I'm having a relaxing meal in a restaurant, or I'm at home. I like beer a lot. This way if I want to have another one in a few minutes, I'll be fine to drive home. I can even have a third. It doesn't matter," Chad explains.

"Yeah, but do the math," Mike says. "At your weight, you should be fine with even three beers in 90 minutes or so. Besides, you're not the type to go hog wild. Everyone knows that."

"The math is why I stick to nonalcoholic beer," Chad explains. "I know that, as you say, I'd probably be fine—even with as many as three beers. But why risk it? The chances of an accident or, God forbid, an impaired driving arrest or DUI are pretty small; but the costs would be devastating. If I want to get mellow, I'll do it at home, where I don't have to worry."

Mike nods in agreement. Chad is right in every way.

"Well, I'm dying to hear what you thought of my meeting." Chad wants Mike to weigh in immediately. "I about burst an artery when Simone pushed back so hard on me over that customer wanting a faster delivery out of the blue. She's sharp, too. I just don't get it."

"You sure you're ready for this, big shot?" Mike is teasing; but he wants to make sure he has Chad's permission to be direct. He is honored Chad asked for his advice. He also wants to give Chad a warning about what is to come.

"Yeah, sure, bring it," Chad says. "That's why we're here."

"Simone is right; and your boy Randy looked like the real leader of the team, not you," Mike says.

"I can't believe you're saying that," Chad says. He isn't upset—just mystified. "You heard the debate. When we break our production discipline, we lose margin. That bid was based on him waiting his turn. If we move Rob Nicholson up in the pecking order, we're screwing up the operation. Even with the extra money he agreed to pay, we can't catch up with the discounts we'll lose on material purchasing. The numbers don't lie. That's why I started to throw a fit."

"Okay, man: Here's my headline for you. When you live only by the holy grail of numbers and make all your decisions dealing with customers, vendors, and staff based on a spreadsheet, you are really *killing* your reputation throughout the company. I call it professional equity. It's how people perceive your ability to get the job done. Right now your job is to lead; and you're not living up to your potential. I can see why you got blasted on the 360 last week. It's obvious. I'm your friend, and I'm telling you those criticisms are valid."

6:20 Chad Wants to Hear More

"Wow. So I really suck as a boss, huh? I should send my diplomas back and ask for a refund." Chad looks straight at his beer and starts methodically wiping the sweat off the glass with his index finger.

"Self-loathing, party of one, your table is now ready!" Mike gives Chad a friendly punch to the bicep. "This pity party doesn't suit you at all, man. You'll get through this as soon as you realize what I have. You have more desire and more energy than anyone else in the company. Figure things out short term and you'll become the rock star that everyone sees in you."

"Yeah, and you can see from today how much professional success that's bringing me." Chad is still looking at his beer.

"Hey, if you don't stop acting like a nerdy high school senior who just caught his prom date making out with the quarterback, I'm going to go home to my loving wife, leave you with the check, and never tell you my little secret to getting you out of that little trough you're in. I can see what's wrong, and what you can do about it."

"Okay, okay. I'll stop whining, I promise. I *definitely* want to hear what you have to say," Chad says.

"Here's the deal, Sunny Jim: Both you and I have been victims of our own early success," Mike says. "We're both really good at specific skills that every boss needs. We've realized it along the way, mostly through compliments from others. We're both on track, careerwise, at a relatively early age. Making the most of what we're good at has helped move us along nicely. Our strengths got us to this point. But continuing full throttle with those strengths can stall and then push our careers backward if we aren't careful."

"I know where you're going with this," Chad says. "You know, I've heard the whole 'strengths become your weaknesses' thing before, Mike."

"Then stop acting like a poster child for the theory," Mike says.

"Am I *that* bad?" asks Chad.

"Yeah; but so am I. Every successful person hits this speed bump. It's just a matter of what you do about it," Mike says. "You're already starting to feel this pain, long before you face any serious consequences. The 360 did its job. Now you're receptive to change; and you're better off than you think you are."

"I seriously hope you're not goofing on me right now, because I don't know anyone who's in great shape after an eight-hour visit with the colorectal surgeon. That's exactly what this day has felt like," Chad says.

"I didn't say you felt *good*; I can see that you don't. What I said was you are in better shape than you think you are. Sure, you look like crap once again; but looks can be deceiving, now can't they?" Mike smiles and pats Chad on the shoulder. The bit of levity helps.

The server appears. "Another round, gentlemen?"

"Sure," Chad says.

"Yes; but make mine just like his," Mike says.

"Great. Two nonalcoholic ambers coming right up." The server moves on.

"Okay, Mr. Charisma. Tell me how your strengths ever hurt you," Chad says.

6:30 Mike Owns Up to His Failures

Over their second beer, Mike tells him. He admits he was always better at interaction than analysis. He loved getting to know other people—anybody, really—and, in turn, having them get to know him. He had mastered the ability to tell quick and interesting stories about himself and then help the other person—even a stranger—to do the same. An ordinary conversation with anyone else could turn into a fascinating conversation with Mike. Everyone said he was a great guy. And they were right—he was. The problem was that he became well aware of his reputation.

"Most important, I liked being liked. So I kept going with what I was good at: meeting people, learning from them, and having them learn from me. Gaining personal acceptance was a driving force for me," Mike explains. He told Chad about how it went all the way back to high school. He had lots of friends and plenty of activities to keep him busy, but he never got more than one or two As a year on his report cards. He wound up going to a state school and working part-time on and off campus. He graduated with middling grades but had an outstanding resume of community and real-world experience. Also, his letters of recommendations from deans, employers, and professors more than made up for the Bs and Cs in his business curriculum.

He got an entry-level job in a marketing group at the company where he and Chad met. He was promoted regularly, which surprised no one. His gift of connecting quickly with everyone he met made for great relationships with vendors, clients, and colleagues; this, despite the fact he generally paid little attention to the details of business. That meant that he double-booked meetings every now and then and even missed an assignment or two. But he was always able to make it right with extra hard work at the last minute—along with his considerable ability to put others at ease and have them enjoy the process.

"Then I became the boss of the division—and I started to get hammered, almost daily. I was concentrating so hard on winning the hearts and minds of my employees I never worked at all on the other things it takes to be a good boss." Mike takes a breath and sips his new beer. He admits to Chad that it tastes pretty good.

"I didn't do nearly enough homework on important financial issues. I was not direct in telling my employees when they were performing poorly and what they could do about it. I'd make an overly gentle nudge and hope that they'd get to where they needed to get because of our tremendous professional relationship. It was dumb—running on a smile and lack of detailed analysis. I was seriously starting to fail for the first time because I was relying too much on what got me here: the fact I knew I could connect with anybody. My strength had become my weakness. The employees may have really enjoyed having me as their boss; but not enough of them were succeeding."

Mike jogs Chad's memory. "Very quickly after I became the boss, the division slowed down in growth. There was a lot of discontent and a ton of whining everywhere I looked. And it was all happening so fast. Sure, the employees said good things about me; but they weren't doing their jobs very well. I wondered what the heck was going on. How could this be happening to me?"

"Yeah, I do remember that you guys were struggling for a while," Chad breaks in. "But it sure didn't last long. Well, whatever; you took care of things quickly. You guys are rockin' all your numbers now. What made you change your approach to being a boss?"

"It was the same thing that's turned on the lightbulb for you. I got a lousy 360 early on, and I vowed it would be the last one I would ever get. I started making wholesale changes," Mike says.

"Like what?" Chad asks.

"Well, there's not enough beer in this joint for me to go into everything, but I'll give you the headlines. I'd made a career out of being able to connect with anybody. But I was not a strong enough leadership communicator to be a good boss. It's made a world of difference." Mike takes another sip of his beer.

"My biggest victory so far has been toning down the pats on the back. It's a difficult struggle, but I've trained myself to compliment less readily these days. And when I *do* hand out praise, I use a lot more detail than I used to. That's far better leadership. My employees know they're getting complimented for quality performance—not because I'm trying to make them feel good about themselves or me."

This answers one of the questions Chad had from Mike's production meeting.

"Is that why you didn't give Jake a golf clap? He had a pretty good report during the production meeting about more upcoming work from that one client," Chad asks.

"Yeah, that's right. Golf claps are for superior performance on something significant. Jake's report was positive; you're right. A couple of years ago, I would have whooped it up over the new Hearthstone projects. Now, I hold it in. Jake's news was good, but I expect good news from competent professionals. I'll go nuts when someone gives *great* news in front of me," Mike says. "But you missed the *real* point. I don't call for golf claps; that's Kim's job. It's her meeting."

Mike explains that he lets his managers lead all group meetings. He preps them beforehand and then critiques their performance later. He wants his managers to really *manage* in a wide variety of situations. Along the way he helps them develop their own powerful communication skills. That means he has to watch from the sidelines—even when he knows he could help in many different situations. He says it takes discipline and hard work to coach others instead taking charge of every problem.

"So that's why you didn't commit to helping Rebecca and Kim with that crazy client?" Chad asks. "I thought for sure you'd come to the rescue."

"You know me too well. I *wanted* to; in fact, it took every fiber of my being not to agree to visit with the client. But I resisted," Mike admits. "It's Kim's job to help Leslie do her job.

Neither is succeeding right now, where, you're right, I probably could. But, instead of bailing them out, I decided to give them direction and see if they could turn it around."

"Isn't that risky? What if it blows up altogether?" Chad asks.

"It doesn't matter," Mike says. "It has to play out this way. I have to get Kim's communication skills more refined so she can be a better boss for Leslie."

Mike pauses and taps his index finger on the table for emphasis. "Look, I like my job. But I'm looking forward to the next challenge as well," Mike says. "The bosses will keep moving me up when they can see that we're not only performing well, but that my team knows what they're doing."

"For a guy who can barely make sense of a column of more than three numbers, you're pretty smart," Chad says. It is the highest praise that Chad bestows.

"Well, that's exactly why I had you come to my meeting," Mike says. "I'm tired of wearing a dunce hat and having my team suffer because our reports aren't very strong. I loved the detail and the tie-ins I saw in your meeting. I'm over ignoring my weaknesses. Can you give me some guidance?" Mike asks.

6:40 Mike Gives Chad a Lesson

"Whoa, I thought we were concentrating on my problems, not your minuscule ones," Chad says. "I'm dying here, crying in my nonalcoholic beer. You give me some 'great boss' tips first; and then we'll get to you."

"Fair enough. Okay, first of all, let's take a look at the Simone thing with the customer who had the audacity to request an early delivery. It's a great example of how your strength is starting to kill your performance," Mike says. "Your command of your financials—heck, *everyone's* financials—is awesome. Your grasp of the flow of cash through your organization would make the accounting teachers I had in college green with envy. But now you gotta let that brilliance rest for a while. The money is in the real world, not in the spreadsheets. A good customer wanted his stuff early. You shouldn't have battled Simone on it to begin with; and then you fought Randy on a great solution. Where's the money in that?"

"It's there because customers screw us up when they break their agreements and ask for special treatment. How can we be profitable if we let customers walk all over us?" Chad counters.

"Your love of the numbers is killing your ability to be flexible. You can be right all the time and still lose money. Besides, I could argue that you aren't really looking at your precious numbers at all. If you were, you'd see that the top number—sales—is the start of the P&L and all cash flow. When you summarily reject a customer's reasonable but messy request, you're begging them to look elsewhere. So you might lose them; and then I'd say congratulations, Chad, you kept your margin but lost future revenue. I didn't go to Kellogg like you did, but I still know a good margin on zero revenue is still zero gross revenue and zero profits. You are great at numbers; now work at being good at seeing things from the other guy's point of view. Maybe with some better coaching from you, Randy would have told Simone to ask for a 6 percent bump and you'd be a little better off. You let your team down when you concentrate on your strengths only. Your weakness is communication. Create powerful connections with your team the way you connect with your friends. Get busy on that."

Chad looks down at his beer. Mike is right. Chad thinks about how the blowup with Phil was completely unnecessary. He had wasted time and jeopardized his good standing with

Lynne by firing off the e-mail so quickly. Phil is a good employee, and he had alienated him. But Chad can't help but complain.

"Yeah, but what's right is right—isn't it?" he asks. "I mean, I never make a case for something unless I'm absolutely certain of the facts. You know that about me."

"Then work from home as an analyst and never talk to anybody. Just crunch numbers and e-mail reports," Mike scolds Chad. "But if you want to be a leader and a boss you have to take the time to communicate clearly, with power and impact. That's a lot more than just small talk; I've learned that firsthand. You spend too much time on making sure you're right and not enough convincing others why you *are*. That takes patience, coaching, and a sincere interest in your employees," Mike says.

"Well, I'm not ever going to be a Netflix buddy with any of my managers like you are with Louis. That's just not me." Though Chad is coming around, he is still pouting.

"And I'm never going to be as efficient with my time as you are. But that's not my goal. My leadership is suffering because I show up to meetings late and unprepared. I asked for help . . . from you, and you delivered quickly. I'm starting sessions with a time-management coach next week. I will get better. Not as buttoned down as you, but better. You can do it, too. It doesn't take huge intellect; it just takes desire to improve."

"Okay, so how do I get a personality injection, if that's what I need?" Chad asks. "Are there ways to get some coaching for better leadership communication?"

"I'll start asking around for you." Mike takes out his Black-Berry and makes a note. If Chad wasn't so focused on his own issues, he would be shocked. Mike *rarely* wrote things down and never in his BlackBerry; he simply wouldn't take the time to learn how to do it. This is a new Mike. Chad has rubbed off on him!

"In the meantime," Mike continues, "put down *Forbes* and *The Economist* for a few weeks, and start reading about building better connections at work. There's a ton of stuff out there on that. You gobble information up; read a book a week from various communications gurus for the next quarter, and you'll start to develop some new skills. Some of the ideas won't appeal to you, but a few will stick with every book you finish. You'll become more flexible and open—just because you'll be working at it. Team that up with your financial horsepower, and you'll be a force."

"Yeah, okay, I can do that," Chad says, "but I want to be better *right now*. Give me some quick tips from the Mike school of connection brilliance."

The server walks up to them. "Another round here?" she asks.

They both look at their watches. Mike shakes his head "no."

"I think we're wrapped up here. Make sure I get the check," Chad says.

"Thanks man, that's very nice. We could have split it," Mike says.

"Oh, I'm going to get my money's worth. So come on, cough up a tip that will help me tomorrow, right away. You know I'll take it seriously," Chad says.

"Okay, here you go: one tip coming up. But next week I buy and we spend the whole time talking about sprucing up my production spreadsheets," Mike says.

6:45 Chad Listens to Mike

Mike tells Chad to take start taking every interaction seriously . . . even ones that don't seem to count for much of
anything. Mike gives him the exact protocol: Ask a few nonintrusive questions and offer up some nonintense personal
information of your own. Chad protests that it would waste
time if he did that all day long. Mike smiles and informs him
that he'd be able to make it up in a hundred different ways.
"Work at your connections all day, every day, and you'll be a
better boss," Mike says.

Chad promises he will, and Mike is impressed with his will-
ingness to learn. He knows he will succeed. The two friends
shake hands and get in their cars.

Chad sees he missed a call from him wife, so he sticks in his
Jawbone and clicks her number.

"Hi, honey; what's up?" Chad asks.

"I never got a chance to get to the dry cleaners to pick up
my suit for tomorrow. Can you get it on the way home?" she
asks.

"Yeah, but it's just about seven. I don't think they're going
to be open," Chad says.

"No, on Mondays and Thursdays they stay open 'til eight.
You should be fine."

Chad agrees and heads for the strip mall near his house. He
deliberately keeps his CD player off and tries to concentrate on
what Mike has told him. He parks his car in front of the dry
cleaners and walks in the door. The woman from this morning
is still at the counter. He is shocked.

"Hi, I need to pick up a suit for my wife. I don't have the
ticket, though . . ."

Joan interrupted him, "Oh, I know who you are. I'll grab your wife's suit right away for you. I'm so sorry I didn't give it to you early this morning when you came in. I could have saved you a trip." Joan says.

"No, it was my fault," Chad says as he hands Joan his debit card. "You can't get something if you don't ask you for it."

"Well, you and your wife have been good customers for quite a while," Joan says. "My husband and I appreciate your business. I should have caught it; I'm sorry again."

"It's not a problem, really," Chad turns to go and then stops and turns back around to face Joan.

"Say, I'm wondering why you stay open an extra hour Monday and Thursday nights."

"Well, the bottom line is that we make more money," Joan says. She explains that she and her husband have been in the dry cleaning business for over 10 years and had experimented with the profitability of various store hours. The Monday/Thursday plan was a real winner for them. A surprising number of clients took advantage of the extra hour; and the volume more than paid for the labor and operating costs. Joan's afternoon employee was on vacation, which explained why she was still at the store.

"You know, I constantly play with the hours of operation and labor costs as well in my job," Chad says. "It's a never-ending process; but I love it." He spends the next few minutes talking about his position and some of the cost-versus-revenue formulas he encountered. Joan is a quick study. She asks several strong questions.

"Well, I should probably introduce myself. My name is Chad." He sticks out his hand.

"And my name is Joan. Tell your wife I said hello. Oh, and one more thing. We're going to be mailing out some coupons tomorrow for a discount on shirts we'll be doing next month. Let me give you a few now so you can take advantage of it early. You can use them right away."

"Wow, thanks Joan. I'm glad I stopped by," Chad says.

"I'm glad you did, too," says Joan.

Boy did I read him wrong, Joan thought to herself as Chad left the store. *He's a pretty nice fellow after all. I bet he does well being a boss at work.*

Chad has his own thoughts as he drives home. *That wasn't bad at all. In fact it was very pleasant; and coupons were a nice touch on her part. I've got to report to Mike first thing in the morning that he's right; I can do this.*

He turns on the radio to light jazz for the short ride home. *Mike is one hell of a sharp stick—a lot sharper than me,* he admits to himself. *Despite the fact he still can't even copy and paste formulas in Excel.*

6:00 PM

Don't Be That Boss Lessons

6:01 Chad Loosens Up

✓ Continue efforts to connect with your employees all day long.

6:15 Mike Starts In

✓ Lead by example in demonstrating flexibility when evaluating customer requests.

(continued)

(*continued*)

6:20 Chad Wants to Hear More

✓ For every boss—*and* employee—strengths have the potential to become weaknesses that will lead to poor performance.

6:30 Mike Owns Up to His Failures

✓ Bosses who develop new strengths can improve performance quickly.

6:40 Mike Gives Chad a Lesson

✓ Successful leaders always have strong communication skills.

6:50 Chad Listens to Mike

✓ Great bosses hone their communication skills every chance they get.